By the same author

The Mimosa and the Mango

To Clive

with best wishes

from

Suzanne St Albans

21 . 1 . 76

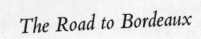

The Road to Bordeaux

The Road to Bordeaux

The Duchess of St Albans

W. H. ALLEN · LONDON
A division of Howard & Wyndham Ltd
1976

Once more it is entirely due to the continual encouragement (not to say downright pressurising) of my noble spouse that this book was written. All blame is to be firmly laid at his door.

I

WHAT WOULD HAVE become of us, marooned on our Provençal hillside with retarded peasant children and homicidal maniacs as sole companions, had not my mother decided at the crucial moment to transfer us to the Atlantic coast, I dread to think.

I suppose there would have been a dreary succession of governesses, no school, no friends, and we would inevitably have grown into unmitigated freaks. Adjusting ourselves to life was bad enough anyway when we came up against it, but nothing to what it would have been if it hadn't caught up with us in the nick of time, and not a moment too soon. As it was, Marie, our one-eyed Swiss nanny, held full sway until I was eighteen, and she would have done so until her death, had not the war snatched us from her grasp when it did. Moreover, we would never have been allowed to have friends to stay, nor to go off on visits ourselves—gallivanting around as my father, with his mania for solitude, and his horror of strangers, used to say. As for education, all you needed, according to him, was to read the *Encyclopaedia Britannica*, which occupied a whole bookcase in his study, learn Latin from the village priest, and any other language which Marie had to offer. School, therefore, was considered quite unnecessary, and the sort of place where you were desperately unhappy and caught everything that was going. But thank goodness Papa, buried as he was in his Malayan jungle, spent years on end away from home, thus allowing Mamma to heed the little flashes of inspiration which descended on her from time to time. And, mercifully, it was owing to one of these welcome flashes that we were eventually moved lock, stock and barrel to the Atlantic coast. But the final transfer did not take place in one fell swoop. We went there several times for the summer months before we settled in St Georges altogether.

The train journey from Nice to Bordeaux took all night at that time (and perhaps it takes even longer nowadays). But we arrived in good order, and the *Chef de Gare* at the little station at Royan, who had been alerted on the telephone by the Nice station master, was on the platform to meet us. Our luggage was hoisted on to a caravan of horse-drawn carriages. We climbed into the first, a *calèche* of ancient design with tufts of horsehair sprouting from the seats, while the tattered remains of the hood flapped in the breeze. Rubio, still clutching the case of table silver with which he had been entrusted, climbed into the second carriage and promptly fell asleep.

'The sea is a little rough today,' remarked the coachman, as we shambled along beside it. The dark green water swung into the bay in one huge mass, edged with breakers as high as horses, galloping along the beach. The tide was coming in, and the huge waves hurled themselves at the sand with a fury and violence we had never seen before. Dead jellyfish as large as bicycle wheels, left over from the previous tide, were lifted up and floated away, to be churned and pounded by the next breaker. How could anyone bathe and paddle in such a raging turmoil?

'It will be much calmer in the Baie de St Georges,' added the coachman, 'it is more sheltered there.'

And so it was, to our relief. When we arrived in the village at the height of the shopping hour with the market in full swing, our convoy, shambling into the main street, created an unexpected stir. We found this puzzling, as we didn't consider we looked any different from our usual ordinary selves, if anything a little on the tidier side (before leaving the train Marie had scrubbed and brushed us down) and we all sat up primly in our white linen hats, while Mamma looked most fetching in a cloche, and Marie no less forbidding than usual. It was obviously Rubio who was letting us down. Fast asleep in his barouche he lay slumped on his seat with his bristly red face squashed onto his chest, his beret over his eyes and the box of table silver firmly clasped in his arms. After him three more carriages followed with the luggage, and on top of the last one, wobbling rather ominously were half a dozen mouse-traps strung together in a shapeless bundle, and our two Singer sewing machines (in case one broke down), both of which are still in my possession in perfect working order, one in Vence and one in London. And when the Singer men who turn up from time to time to do the maintenance nag away at me to swap my elegant vintage treasures for the squat and hideous model of current design, they obviously think me quite mad to prefer my own. On one or two occasions when, without thinking, I muttered reminiscently, 'They always used to sit on top of the luggage with the mouse-traps,' the poor man shot me a look of alarm, snapped his toolbox shut and departed in haste. So now I try to remember to keep my mouth shut.

The chalet Gaudin had been described by the agents as a large family residence full of old-world charm. The operative word was certainly old. In fact it was crumbling. When our convoy brought us to the gate we thought we had arrived at the Sleeping Beauty's castle. You could hardly see the house for trees. They towered above the roof, creepers and vines swarmed all over the walls, and the wide front steps sweeping up to the terrace on the first floor were shrouded in ferns and mosses. Great loops of cobwebs hung about like washing lines, and some of the shutters hung on one hinge, while others were encrusted into the walls like barnacles. The vapours of the ocean, Marie said, were the cause of it all.

Rubio, who was still fast asleep in the second carriage, was now prodded awake by the coachman, who poked him in the ribs with his whip.

'Come on you lazy bones, and give us a hand with the luggage,' he grumbled. Unloading our bags and cases was no joke. Apart from the actual trunks full of bed and table linen, and kitchen utensils which Marie had thought essential to bring, the luggage piling up in the garden included camp beds, a field medical chest, a large box containing photographic developing equipment, a trunk filled with toys, games and books, and, perched on top of the lot, sat the two Singer sewing machines, and a swing for Rubio to hang in the garden for us.

The chalet, as it called itself, was decorated with decayed fretwork and built on no intelligible plan. Even in summer, as we soon found out, it was damp and dark as a dungeon. The back bedrooms had trees growing in through the windows, and any light which might have filtered into the dining-room was extinguished by the network of creepers which enveloped the house. It was like the twilit gloom of an aquarium.

A long stone passage led to the only loo, which seemed a terrible bore at first, but this distance soon revealed itself as a blessing in disguise as the days passed and the time approached for the visit of M. le Vidangeur. When he finally arrived, driving his stinking, creaking lorry through the garden, and inserted a pump into a square of cement behind the house, we fled out of the house with cries of protest. The poor man's pride was deeply wounded and I heard him say to my mother as she dived out of the house with a handkerchief over her face, 'it is a profession as honourable as any other'.

The garden, mysterious and creepy, was full of narrow tunnels between box hedges, ancient cedars with immense branches snaking along the ground, and a variety of trees and ferns, so tangled with vines and ivy that it looked as if it had been abandoned for a hundred years. The overall atmosphere was one of languor and melancholy decay. All this luxuriant vegetation would at least, I thought, shelter an abundant insect life, which would surely keep Marie happy.

A wall, seven or eight feet high, separated us from the garden next door, which sloped down to the beach, and which was the stamping ground of a little girl whose legs were in irons and whose skull had been split open in four equal parts. The doctors, who thought that her leg trouble resided in her brain, had insisted on the operation. Inordinately proud of her scars, she would crane her shorn head at us, showing off the pink stitched seams in the shape of a cross. Perched on top of the wall we would peer down, fascinated by the magnificently extravagant scars. Sometimes, at her invitation, we slithered down on her side of the wall, but as the poor creature could neither run nor climb trees, there wasn't much future in the friendship. Drunk and giddy with the glory of heights, we spent most of our time in the trees. From the top of the wall it was literally child's play to swing into the cedars, and from there to proceed all the way round the garden, cruising along the treetops, creeping from branch to branch in the lime-green twilight like a troop of monkeys. Completely invisible from the ground, we took great care to keep dead quiet, as our treetop life was like another world, a glorious in-between state, neither subject to the rigours of earthly discipline, nor the ascetic standards of heaven. Sometimes Marie would stamp about below, calling and searching, with the broad brim of her hat flapping up and down in mounting irritation.

One fine day we decided to build a house of our own up

there and become permanent citizens of those upper regions.

It took a long time to carry the boards up and nail them down into a firm platform which is, after all, all it was. Sometimes we tied a ground sheet to the branches above, but we so much preferred to see the sky through the leaves that we soon gave up the roof altogether. All the time that we were not on the beach, or climbing about on the reef, we spent in our tree house. Usually we managed to get up there while no one was looking, but we were once caught at it by Christine, who was then old enough to totter around, but certainly not old enough to climb trees.

'Nette (which was how she always referred to herself) want to go up too,' she announced on that occasion. We said no, that it was too high and she would fall out. She insisted, and we told her to run away and play. Whereupon she let out a piercing yell. 'Nette going to tell Marie.' The little pest was going to sneak, and that would be the end of our tree life. I slithered to the ground and ran to the woodshed to collect a basket, and tying a rope to the handle, I scrabbled up the tree again with the rope in my teeth. We started to haul her up. All went well at first. Suddenly the basket began to swing from side to side.

'Nette don't like it,' she whined. The basket was now half way up and the swinging increased. Suddenly it banged heavily against the tree and Christine let out another penetrating screech.

'Shut up,' ordered John, 'or we'll drop you.' As the rope grew shorter, the whole arrangement acquired a spin. In a few seconds it was whizzing round like a catherine-wheel.

'Nette going to be sick,' she whimpered as she reached our level.

'Don't you dare be sick,' growled John, 'you're here now, so stop fussing.' She was jammed underneath the boards, and the harder we pulled, the more we flattened the poor creature into her basket.

'We've got to get her *over* the edge,' I kept saying, 'we can't just pull her *through* the floor !' In the end, we managed to haul her on board, by manœuvring her swiftly up and over, as she came into view on a forward swing. When she eventually crawled out of her basket she was white as new snow, and quivering ominously. I took her on my lap and smoothed her down, while John was tying the rope around her middle, hooking the other end on to a branch. Thus firmly tethered, she was allowed to roam at will.

'If you fall overboard we can yank you back,' John told her comfortingly. 'But try not to, all the same.'

After that episode we always took great care to shin up our tree when we knew Christine to be well out of range.

On very hot days, Marie, who hated the sand, the sun and the sea, marched us firmly off to the forest behind the sand dunes. There she settled under some vast oozing pine, which spewed resin from every pore, as its fumes, inhaled into our tubes, would keep off winter colds and wheezes. In Vence she frequently made us play in the shade of eucalyptus trees for the same reason. And there she sat, happily knitting away our endless winter socks, clicking and flashing her four steel pins at an incredible rate while we mooned around, bored to death and longing for the beach. If we were lucky enough to have settled down by an ants' nest, all was well and the day was saved. Another powerful attraction were the caterpillar processions with thousands of individuals crawling along nose to tail in single file for miles on end. Marie would even put her knitting aside for these, and go down on hands and knees, peering sideways at the creatures which humped along in total unconcern. Occasionally she fished out one of her specimen bottles and scooped up a handful to take home for pickling purposes.

Growing all round among the pine needles were huge thick fleshy flap mushrooms, each one as large and heavy and solid as a pound of steak and deliciously indigestible when fried in olive oil with chopped garlic and parsley. But Marie, who didn't trust them, wouldn't have them in the house, so we just kicked off their heads and watched the quantities of worms wriggling angrily out of the stalks.

Due to her regrettable thumb-sucking habit, Anne's second batch of teeth which had just arrived on the scene, were beginning to poke forward in an alarming way. Whether intentionally or not, she was beginning to damage people with them. They were razor-sharp, and she was becoming dangerous. From time to time you could hear John growling angrily, 'Do be careful, you've hit me with your teeth again.'

'I can't help it,' she would wail in reply, 'they stick out too far in front of me.'

'Well, keep your mouth shut, then.'

'I can't, my lips won't meet. It's not my fault,' and she would burst into tears.

In the end, Mamma took the matter in hand, and Anne went to visit a special dentist in Royan, who fitted her up with a horrific flesh-coloured bakelite contraption. This consisted of two sections which could be eased apart gradually as the roof of her mouth widened under the pressure. This gruesome-looking instrument was held together with a collection of tiny screws and silver wires, which became known, naturally enough, as Anne's cleft palate. She was supposed to wear it day and night, but as she couldn't speak through it, she had to spit it out into a handkerchief every time she wanted to utter. Half the time of course, the wretched thing was found lying around in the most unlikely places, and from time to time you could hear someone shouting, 'Anne, your palate's fallen down behind the dresser,' or 'for God's sake take this ghastly thing away,' as you found it nestling in your pencil box, or in the table-napkin drawer in the dining-room. And, occasionally, when my mother did one of her swift and totally unpredictable pounces into our midst, she would demand, 'Where's your palate? Why aren't you wearing it? Go and find it at once.' Poor Anne's life was unmitigated

[8]

misery during those palate years. On one occasion as we were all sitting down to lunch, a loud crunching sound was suddenly heard under the table.

'Who's given Sam a bone?' asked my mother sternly. 'You know he mustn't be fed at meals.' (Sam was a black cocker spaniel who had come to live with us after some slight difference of opinion with his own family, the Hilliers.)

As we were eating skate and black butter at the time we could all claim, quite truthfully, that none of us was guilty of giving Sam a bone.

'He's probably scratched one out of his store in the garden,' John remarked placidly. Everybody knew that Sam had several of these larders, all in various degrees of odoriferous putrefaction at various chosen spots in the garden. Peering under the table we bent down in unison to remonstrate with him. Sam glared at us all in turn and suddenly Anne wailed, 'It's my palate!'

'Really!' exploded Mamma, 'this is too much! Why on earth did you give it to him?'

'I didn't give it to him' whimpered Anne. 'He must have pinched it out of my pocket.'

'Well, get it back at once! I've never heard of such a thing!' My mother, whose neck was growing red with annoyance, was beginning to work herself up. As Anne went down on her knees under the table, Sam uttered a deep growl of warning.

'He likes it,' remarked John. 'He won't give it up. He's never had anything so tasty before.'

'Don't be so disgusting,' said Mamma, 'and do be careful Anne, he might bite.'

'Of course he won't bite,' I said indignantly, 'Sam never bites.'

Anne crept forward another inch, and Sam's lips curled back to a snarl as he fluffed out his feathers. We held our breath as they glared at each other, their eyeballs protruding. This seemed likely to go on forever. It was stalemate. Suddenly my nerve gave and I exploded in a violent sneeze. Sam gave a little jump and Anne pounced on her palate.

'I've got it,' she yelled in triumph, reappearing at table level.

'Well go and disinfect it at once,' commanded Mamma. 'Ask Marie for some of her pickling spirits and make sure it's completely clean.'

When we next saw the object it was residing in state in a jam jar full of spirits, between a pickled grass snake and a four-legged chicken on the top shelf of the kitchen dresser. And after a suitable length of time it was duly reinstated in poor Anne's mouth.

2

IN SPITE OF the darkness and the smells, our first summer in St Georges was pure bliss. For three hot months we lived on a beach of white sand four miles long, we paddled and shrimped and 'swam' in the shallows with one foot on the bottom, and so gentle were the waves that we did not even have to wear our lifebelts. (Rubber rings, wings and suchlike were still inventions of the future at that time.)

The only fly in the ointment was the daily gym lesson on the sands.

After our usual breakfast of cocoa and bread and butter, we were trotted down to the beach, where M. Coulon, the gym master, marshalled us and the children from the surrounding villas into lines and columns like a battalion in training. Running, jumping, skipping, standing on our hands, whatever he did strutting in front, blowing his whistle like the Pied Piper, we had to copy. For a whole hour he marched us about, forming squares, circles, stars, set-pieces, with other children standing on top of us, digging their toe-nails into our shoulders, or balanced on their heads, resting their feet on our chins. At the end of the lesson he chased us all into the sea, to pick out those who sank from the ones who could swim. The latter he left to their own devices, but he pulled out the sinkers and flung them on the beach, after which, as we were in the second category, he had a private word with my mother about swimming lessons.

M. Coulon told her that we would undoubtedly drown before the end of the summer unless we had lessons, and she naturally fell for this.

After lunch, for which we returned to our sombre villa, came the siesta on the beach. Mamma made us lie flat on our backs, stripped to the waist, and popping seaweed on to our chests, she rubbed the slimy jelly into the skin. This, as everybody knew, being full of iodine and other precious minerals, would be baked into the bloodstream by the sun, thus keeping coughs and colds and wheezy chests away for the whole winter. Then, when done on one side, we were turned over for basting and roasting on the other. How she managed to keep up this boring performance for a whole summer I cannot imagine. But I suppose that her reward came the following winter when we caught nothing worse than measles, plus a dose of pneumonia for myself.

Moved by one of her sudden flashes of inspiration, on which she always acted immediately without a second's hesitation or reflection, Mamma had decided to bring us to St Georges because it was the home of her friends Pierre and Camille Darlange, whom she had known in Malaya at the time of her marriage. My birth had come a few months after their own son's arrival, and we had often been trundled together in the same pram under the banana trees, and presumably received our bedtime whiff of chloroform from the same bottle.

The parents of Pierre Darlange had lived at Nostram, an old house in the middle of the village, since the beginning of time. They were very old. And their own children, of whom there were six, had a great number of children of their own, all of whom converged on St Georges every summer, and Nostram, crammed to the attics, seemed inexhaustibly expansible. It was a very large household. The Darlange children, our contemporaries, built on a large scale, were twice as big as we were, and I suspect that my mother, secretly envious of her friends' brood of giants, submitted us to those daily gym lessons on the beach in an effort to stretch us upwards and sideways as much as possible. But I regret to say that although we were put through this infinitely dreary performance for many years, she was defeated in her purpose and we remained as we were, growing at our own leisurely pace, and as thin as stick insects. But day after day, with agonising self-consciousness, we staggered through our antics, knowing that we were being watched by our friends, who sat patiently waiting for us in the dunes until we were free.

To have friends on tap at all times, whom we could meet freely on the beach, as it were on neutral ground, was a new and exhilarating experience, and we made the most of it. We became inseparable, a close-knit pack, like a shoal of fish, all moving instinctively together in the same direction, as if governed by a corporate brain. And when we had to part for meals, and to go to bed at night, it was just as painful as it is for lovers to be separated.

When we tired of bathing and building sand castles, we clambered over the reef which was left uncovered at low tide. Thickly carpeted with the bladder-wrack which Mamma popped on our chests, it was very slippery, and our knees and elbows were continually cut open, but this was nothing compared with the excitement of jumping from rock to rock, and the discoveries we made in the cracks and the pools left behind by the retreating tide. Filled with life of every kind, from sea-spiders to prawns and tiny squids, we never tired of exploring them.

Right on the edge of the reef by the sea was a very large pool, which we knew well. Like a miniature ocean, it contained a selection of deep-sea fauna on a mini scale. There we found the baby flying squid, that intriguing creature which flicked from one end of the pool to the other, and which is said to be quite brainless, though possessing a heart as stout as a power station. I was surprised to learn that the cuttle (the thing which canaries sharpen their teeth on) is set quite loose and slides about at will underneath the animal's gelatine skin. Difficult to capture, they shot out a squirt of ink if a shadow crossed their path, making them invisible at once. Whelks glided through the seaweed, wrapping themselves round any shell they came across, sawing away at it with their long murderous tongue, edged with hundreds of razor-sharp teeth set in rows of three, so that when one snapped off, another rushed forward to take its place. With this kit they had no trouble in boring through the toughest shell and sucking the unhappy mollusc out of his home. Also in this pool, sea-snails grazed in herds among the bladder-wrack, advancing head high in slow and dignified progress, heaving one side forward, then dragging up the other like an obese old woman suffering from her feet, and long tongue, also set with formidable teeth, held at the ready for wrenching the tough weed off the rocks. The common tops, with their pretty shells, were also found in large congregations weaving their way through the undergrowth. Glassy shrimps, their undercarriage loaded with eggs, shot through the water, zigzagging about above the floating tentacles of the sea anemones. When a victim was caught, it was slowly wrapped up and drawn down into the gaping, toothless maw which served as dining-room, kitchen, nursery and waste disposal unit all in one. The anemone, for all its eyeless, mindless state, is a creature organised beyond belief. But although it enjoys a first-class network of nerves, its sex life must be dismally unrewarding. Sometimes in answer to some pre-primordial urge, an individual will suddenly stretch itself like a rubber band until it splits asunder, each half starting again from scratch. Should any fragments drop off at the time of snapping, these will also grow into baby anemones. At other times, again presumably egged on by some mysterious call, they go broody and decide to lay eggs instead of splitting, then proceed to nurse the family within the folds of their stomach pouch. How the eggs avoid being digested along with the latest meal is a mystery we could never solve. As soon as they felt up to it, away they floated with the debris of the last supper, in search of adventure on the high seas. Also trapped in this pool, we often found baby jellyfish waiting for the tide to lift them off and bear them away to deeper waters. At that stage they had only just budded off from their stalk in the polyp colony, which grew along the jetty of the little harbour. For jellyfish are free-living animals only once every other generation. In the swimming stage, trailing poisonous tentacles for fishing purposes, they drop their eggs in the sea leaving the rest to chance, hoping for the best, or more probably not giving a damn. When in the larval stage, they hunt around for a suitable spot to take root and proceed to grow into a polyp, eventually sprouting little shoots which then burgeon into buds, and on breaking off, turn into baby jellyfish. And thus the cycle is complete. It seems a complicated way of going about it all for a simple, unsophisticated thing like a jellyfish, even though it may reach really vast proportions, the largest ever captured being twelve feet across, with tentacles one hundred feet long.

Starfish were really the tigers of the pools and in great numbers everywhere, wriggling along on their neat little tube feet, so numerous that when any of them got tired or damaged in any way, they simply tucked them up and let down a few dozen more to take over. These tiny feet, fitted with powerful suction pads, also came in useful for prising open clams or oyster shells which stubbornly refused to open. The starfish would simply wrap the shell up in its arms, switch on the suction, and use all its feet in rotation until the wretched shell, exhausted by the struggle, simply had to let go. Then, taking the mountain to Mahomet, the starfish would shoot out its stomach, insert it into the shell and wrap it round the occupant, digesting it alive in its own parlour.

Sea-urchins, hidden away among the weed, were a proper menace. It didn't pay to step on them. The spines, hooked on the end like tiny harpoons, would break off in the sole of your foot, and have to be cut out by the chemist. After one of these operations I couldn't walk for a week. But they were nonetheless fascinating creatures, when you think that those murderous spines were only little trouser legs for the creature's feet which slid up and down inside them and stuck out several inches beyond, waving about looking for purchase to draw the clumsy lump along. The mouth, if you could find it, was tucked away somewhere among all those spikes, and fitted with five little protruding teeth for scooping up rubbish along the ocean floor. So you could say they are, in their usefulness, a kind of dung-beetle of the deep.

Sea-cucumbers were another intriguing group—some fat and short, some long and hollow like macaroni. I picked up one of the corpulent type once but dropped it in a hurry as the revolting brute spat all his guts out in my face, which is apparently their mode of self-defence. And in the ensuing confusion they lurch away to knit themselves a whole new set of insides. Another curious creature whose identity I could never discover and which floated about in the larger pools of the reef, looked like a little brown doormat with bristles on both sides of its anatomy. It neither stung nor pricked nor spat when picked up, and in spite of minute examination, I never could find a mouth or any other orifice. We took a couple back to our aquarium, so that we could study them at leisure, but they never gave any of their secrets away.

Small, soft-shelled green crabs crawled about among the seaweed over which thick clouds of sea-fleas jumped up and down in a frenzy of perpetual motion, and seahorses swung about in the deeper pools, as if suspended on a thread, or curled their tails around a seaweed stalk. I never saw them eating anything even though we brought them crumbs, minute water-fleas and any other scraps we could think of. They swam up, nosed at our offerings with their little snouts, and floated away again. Sea-snails crawled about everywhere in profusion and were constantly crunched under foot. We once made a mistake of taking back a jamjar full of them as a present for Marie, only to find the jar empty the next morning, the wretched snails swarming in the sugar, the coffee beans, the bread bin, while the rest were cruising across the ceiling in search of other delights. Sea-lilies clung to the bottom of the deeper pools, waving their delicate petals above their heads, all innocence and fragility. Sea-slugs undulated along the bottom, with two little horns sticking out of the top of their heads like tiny periscopes, and a little feathery tuft on the end of the tail. Another model was camouflaged by a dense growth of bush sprouting all over its back, so it looked like a bit of travelling seaweed.

At very low tide the reef was covered by miles of oyster-beds, with shells as murderous as broken glass which slashed your gym shoes to ribbons. Cemented as they were to the rock, it seemed a dull life for them, their only excitement lying in their annual change of sex, being one year male and the other female, and although crowded in such dense colonies, condemned to the company of their next door neighbours for life, quite unable to move around and see new faces. These oysters were soon to become the plague of my life.

Our sea aquarium (we also had a fresh water one), a model of its kind, was a large wash-tub sunk into the ground in the garden, with a wire fence all round to discourage cats. (Needless to say Marie had already begun to collect the feline population of the district.) The aquarium was a faithful copy of one of the pools in the reef. We had even managed to chip off bits of rock with oysters attached, and these we distributed around the sides, with bladder-wrack and kelp for the seahorses to find anchorage, and to offer protection to the slugs and snails, who never ventured far from its shelter. For the whelks we brought a daily supply of clams, and for the anemones we went shrimping at low tide. The starfish gobbled everything they came across, and the sea-urchins hoovered up the sandy bottom, disposing of shrimp legs and soft crabshells and any other debris available. After my adventure with the sea-cucumber we decided to leave the breed alone, and had two little doormats instead. Tiny soft-shelled green crabs scuttled about everywhere and we even, at one time, had a baby jellyfish, but he vanished overnight, presumably consumed by one of the sea-anemones.

A great pleasure which we enjoyed so to speak second-hand, was fishing. Following the top of the cliff above our reef was a narrow path called the Chemin de la Falaise, where a number of fishermen had a permanent pitch. At high tide they lowered large square nets hanging from a rope, which was wound up and down on a pulley. When the tide began to ebb, we raced to the cliff to inspect the catch of the day. This was always a mixed bag, with quantities of jellyfish predominating. The waters of the bay, nourished as they were by the village drains, sustained a rich and varied marine population. There were sole, crabs, lobsters, grey mullet, dabs and plaice, and sometimes a clutch of drowned new-born kittens. The first time we were given a batch of these by the fishermen, we flew home to resuscitate them, convinced that they were merely in a bad way. Tucked up in cotton wool, we placed them carefully in a wooden box beside the kitchen furnace, and tried to force warm milk into their small, clamped-down mouths. On the third day, the usual day for resurrections, we lost all hope when the little creatures seemed to have shrunk still further into themselves, and Marie declared that she would not put up with these stinking cadavers in her kitchen any longer. So we were forced to bury our poor little corpses.

3

AT THE END of September the Darlange family returned to Paris and we went back to Vence, brown and fit and bursting with ozone and all kinds of essences emanating from the various trees under which we had sat; it may have been due to all those blessings that the attack of measles which struck that winter was quite mild, leaving none of the side effects predicted by Marie, such as total blindness and deafness for life. Moreover, we missed the diphtheria epidemic which raged in Vence after Christmas, wiping out half the child population of the village, including the postman's eight-year-old daughter. This was very sad, as he was a great friend of Marie's. He came from Alsace, and both of them, loathing *les Boches* with their whole hearts as they did, nevertheless throughly enjoyed a daily gossip in German, which was frustrating for us, as we understood no word of what they said. Seated on kitchen chairs under the orange trees, with a bottle of wine on a table between them, they chattered away together while we waited impatiently for the contents of the mailbag to be brought out. This usually took place after a couple of glasses of wine, when the 'Alsatian' fished out the postcards which he read aloud, so that we were always kept in touch with the local news. '*Tiens,*' he would say, pulling out a plum, 'this one is in English. You read it, Madame Marie, and tell us what it is all about.'

When it was in French, he read it out himself: 'Aha, the son of Madame Bichet who is doing his military service in Algeria has had blackwater fever. He says his *caporal* is a pig. I can well believe it!' Or—'The daughter of Madame Cochet has had her baby. A boy weighing three kilos—not bad!' And then once in a while, '*Par example*! Here is one for you, Madame Marie, from one of your step-daughters. You'd better read it yourself,' and he handed it gallantly to her. The letters from foreign parts, with exotic stamps from Mauritius, Madagascar and Cochin-China, they turned over this way and that, holding them up to the sun and peering through the thin airmail envelope, trying at least to decipher the signature. But I never actually saw them opening one. Very disappointing for all of us.

That winter my father came back on leave from Malaya, and Mamma started to agitate again about the dreaded subject of education. It was enough to make anyone ill, and this is exactly what I proceeded to do, in spite of the bladder-wrack, and all the ozone.

During our absence in Malaya our farmer had died, and as the idea of a home farm had lost its charm anyway, my mother summoned Mr Demichelis, who at that time owned the only building firm in Vence, and instructed him to remodel the farm into a 'winter house' (smaller and warmer and easier to run). This became the cause of what seemed to us quite inexplicable fuss. In the Baous, the mountains all round us, there was a pass called *Le Trou de la Dame*, and this was the name which Papa insisted on giving the new house. We simply could not under-stand Mamma's outraged indignation. In the end it was named after the mountain range of the Esterel which it overlooks in the South, and which is the kingdom of the fairy Esterelle, from whom it took its name. The fairy's approval, which we hoped for, was communicated to us the next evening by a blood-red glow hanging over her hills, surrounded by a scarlet halo easing off into an emerald sky. The priest then came up from the village to perform the blessing rites, during which he led us all in solemn procession over the whole house, sprinkling holy water into every corner to drive out the devil and his minions, reciting the appropriate magic words at the same time. We felt the place, after this combination of pagan omens and Christian rites, ought to be safe and bring us luck and happiness for ever-more. Little did we know that it would, in fact, become a thorn in our flesh, and that the curse which Esterelle, whose message we must have misunderstood, had put on it was there for all time, and that none of us for all our efforts would ever be able to break it.

As the distance between the houses is less than a hundred yards, the move was simply a matter of running back and forth with loads of clothes, silver, bedding and kitchen utensils. We were naturally press-ganged into the operation, spending the rest of the day staggering up and down the path like pack-mules, dumping our loads in the new kitchen where Marie was floundering about trying to bring order into the monumental muddle.

Soon after we moved in, a great flood washed right through the house during a thunderstorm, while Mamma and I, en-grossed in our books, sat curled up on the drawing-room sofa, completely oblivious to what was going on around us, until the floating rugs began to spin about the room. So perhaps after this the house was damp, or the thought of an impending new governess was too much, anyway down I went with pneu-monia, and the hens got chicken-pox in sympathy. They were dosed with sulphur, and I was submitted to the horrors of the full treatment. Cupping and bleeding proved ineffective for once, and as I lay on my bed shaking with fever and panting for breath, with tears rolling down my face at the pain in my side,

Marie came in every two hours with an icy, soaking wet sheet. Stripping off my nightdress she clamped this on to me, rolling me up in it like a parcel and growling at me at the same time to stop crying and behaving like a baby. Her philosophy was never to give sympathy, as it only made you feel more sorry for yourself. And I am not sure that she was so very far wrong. Although this may seem like rough treatment, nowadays that pneumonia, thanks to antibiotics, is hardly worse than a cold, I was lucky compared with the peasant children of my generation. They had to put up with far worse horrors, such as swallowing the juice of crushed live snails mixed with sugar, or having a pigeon split in half, clamped, still palpitating to their heads, or freshly torn-off rabbit skins wrapped round their chests, and worst of all, they continually had to suffer the most dreadful indignities connected with their nether regions. Little pellets, bits of soap, cloves of garlic were pushed up their bottoms, and most astonishing of all, constipation was treated with the insertion of a violet. What happened when violets were out of season leaves one wondering. Whooping cough, when it resisted snail juice, was cured by pushing the child seven times backwards and forwards under the belly of a donkey. Some of these animals were famous for miles around for their curative powers, and the patients were driven to far-distant villages, bumping along the mountain paths in horse-carts for their treatment. But in spite of all this care and trouble, child mortality was very high in those days.

After what seemed like weeks of painful illness, and even more painful treatment, my natural toughness pulled me through and I slowly got better. Papa, whom I hadn't seen since I had taken to my bed, came and sat beside me with a book. This undreamed-of treat made up for everything. He read me the *Divine Comedy* right through to the end, in French. It was utterly delightful to be lying back in bed with a large pipless orange in my lap (an amazing new development of the

[22]

time, and therefore a tremendous treat) and listening to his dear weak voice, while gazing out of the window at the pale spring sky and the olive trees waving slowly from side to side.

When we had squeezed everything we could out of Dante, he read me extracts from a huge tome of Rabelais' complete works, and we both rocked with laughter at the adventures of Pantagruel, Panurge and Gargantua. He was in one of his rare frivolous moods, reading the medieval French with the local *accent du pays*, which made it sound all the funnier.

Then he read Lamb's *Essays of Elia* in English, and the mood changed to one of delicate melancholy. After this I got up and went downstairs, feeling weak and light-headed, and Papa once more withdrew into himself and his study, and from then on, hardly seemed to recognise me when we met in the hall or on the landing.

All this time John and Anne had led a busy and engrossing life *à deux* in the garden, and did not want me either. When I followed them around, trying to hear what they were saying, they whispered together and ran off calling me *cisaille*, which means garden scissors, and although this was a word none of us had ever used before, their meaning was perfectly clear to me: I was no longer wanted. Though we normally spent most of our time together, we still had our own private occupations which we kept quite secret, and when one of us went off with a determined step and a *certain air*, the others kept away and asked no questions. And so I never knew what they were up to when John pottered off with a preoccupied look on his face, or when Anne wandered away vaguely with two hats on her head. My own favourite private occupation demanded a great deal of concentration and was a thoroughly satisfying experience. It consisted of sitting in the fork of a mimosa tree in bloom, and trying *to feel like the tree*. Nothing in the world seemed more delightful than the thought of having sprigs of mimosa sprouting out of your arms and legs and the tips of your fingers. It was really a question of the time available. If you were called away or distracted too soon, nothing much happened, but when a long sunny afternoon stretched ahead, you could be pretty sure of plugging in to the 'tree feeling' fairly quickly, and then your own identity floated away and you became a living part of the tree itself, rippling in the breeze and tingling with all the little thoughts and feelings which came rushing up out of the ground, usually so tenuous and elusive that you could never catch them any other way.

But at this particular time mimosa was out of season, and I was not in the mood for plugging in anyway, so I mooned around by myself, sitting for hours on end on the swing which Rubio had rigged up for us in an olive tree, and munched pomegranates, disconsolately spitting out the pips for the ants to carry away to their babies. Rubio would come and lean against the tree and ask me what the matter was, and bring me presents of baby mice and dead birds, to cheer me up. But it didn't work, and everything seemed out of joint. So in a way it was a relief when the new governess turned up at last.

As spring set in early that year, the move back to the big house for the summer coincided with her arrival, so that her first job was to help us bundle our belongings back to the Mistral, and store them in their rightful places under Marie's eagle eye. I often wondered afterwards what the new governess's feelings must have been when she arrived at the house with her luggage, to be greeted by a mountain of household chattels on the terrace, and her new charges shooting out of the house one after the other with huge loads of blankets, saucepans and silver. When later on she plucked up the courage to ask Marie the reason for this seasonal tidal flow which swept the entire household backwards and forwards from one house to the other twice a year, the curt reply was that 'the children needed a change of air.'

4

MADEMOISELLE POUTOUX WAS quite pleasant and harmless, and I think a little bemused by the abysmal depth of our ignorance. She had probably never come across anything quite like it, and wasn't sure how to tackle the problem. Hoping perhaps to win our co-operation, she did away with the needle-pointed nibs and purple ink, allowing us to use pencils instead. John, being mechanically minded, enjoyed doing sums, nice friendly adding-up with different combinations of the same figures, so that the results were always identical. At that time he had a passion for headgear and was never seen without something on his head. Sometimes it was an old disused work-basket, or a discarded bathing cap with a strap under the chin, but more often than not, he was completely invisible underneath one of Marie's enormous garden hats. As it was always far too big for him, the breeze got hold of the brim, and the whole thing swung back and forth quite freely on his head. With face screwed up over his sums, and short fat fingers uncurling from his left fist to help with the counting, he was quite oblivious of the spinning hat whizzing round his head. But I, with my feeble powers of concentration, found it distinctly distracting to have this thing rotating under my nose, never quite knowing which way round it would go next, and on which side to expect the little black patent leather bow to reappear. As far as my own studies were concerned, I managed with masterly cunning to persuade Mademoiselle Poutoux that nobody could get on in life without an intimate knowledge of the insect population of the district. I must admit that even I was surprised when she fell for it. As a result I spent a lovely lot of time drawing some half-squashed butterfly, specially captured for the purpose, or a bruised stalkless orchid, or a bedraggled moonflower.

On one occasion, as I was allowed as a special treat to choose a subject for my homework, I went to Papa's study and pulled out a heavy gilt-edged mid-nineteenth century tome on natural history, and leafing through it, came across an illustration which looked nice and simple, and yet at the same time deeply satisfying.

Giving my pencil a juicy lick to impart richness to the lead, I got down to work at once, copying the simple outlines into my exercise book. The model being in black and white, I thought I could improve on that, so I filled in my drawing with red and blue, leaving a white stripe in the middle, the brave gay colours of the French flag. This I considered a great improvement on the original, and underneath my drawing when completed, I conscientiously copied out the caption from the book: *Ill. 127 Genitalia of the Robber-Fly.*

Genitalia, what a beautiful poetic word! It would, in fact, make a very suitable name for a doll, unusual yet unpretentious. And there and then I decided to re-christen my walking winking doll, who would in future bear the noble names of Genitalia, Yseult (her present name) Fesq.

Anne, by swivelling her enormous oyster-coloured eyes all round their sockets in an unblinking stare, had learnt the useful trick of hypnotising the governess into letting her get away with murder, or rather with doing nothing at all. So there she sat with her thumb in her mouth steadily pushing out her front teeth, her huge eyeballs rolling about, following Mlle Poutoux's every movement. Lessons on the whole were relaxed and un-eventful and I don't remember a thing I learnt under that régime.

Crawling up and down the garden on hands and knees look-ing for suitable subjects for Mlle Poutoux's lessons, and speci-mens for Marie's pickling bottles, I came across quite a few creatures, some of whose habits were eccentric, to say the least. When I couldn't altogether believe my eyes I would go and check the facts with Papa's natural history book, and in it I discovered the identity of the small maggot who stuck pins into snails and then briskly groomed himself all over with a tiny brush growing out of the end of his tail. This enterprising little fellow was apparently the glow-worm's grub, whose favourite food is a particular variety of snail which he can smell a mile away. When the unfortunate creature finds himself in the grub's firing line, his only defence is apparently to ooze slime from every pore, thus hoping to drown his assailant in the resulting gooey flood. Hence the need for the grub's frantic grooming before and after getting down to his meal.

Another brush-bearing individual was the stag-beetle, of which I once captured a very handsome specimen who was so engrossed in his lunch that he never saw me coming. I carefully brought down my hunting sieve, borrowed from the kitchen for the purpose, over him, slipped a piece of cardboard under-neath, and proudly carried the whole lot to Marie. Sitting under the cherry tree with Christine at her feet, she was knitting winter socks.

'What have you got there?' she asked suspiciously, bringing her good eye down to bear on my trophy.

'A stag-beetle? I've got several of those! And far better ones, too.'

Feeling rather deflated, I was going to take him back to his stamping ground when Marie's eye peered closer. 'Interesting,' she conceded, 'I've never seen one carrying on like that before,' as the creature calmly went on scooping up his juicy pear with a little orange-coloured brush, and shovelling it into his mouth as fast as he could go, as neat as two pins and never dropping the smallest speck. At least *this* was something new to Marie, even if she *had* got better specimens. But needless to say I got no credit for it. Any kind of approval would have been wanton spoiling, 'praise the brat and ruin the child' was one of her favourite home-made mottos, and in all the eighteen years during which she controlled my life, I never got a smile personally meant for me, nor a word of approbation or encouragement. But it was a long time before I gave up trying, currying favour, as she called it, when it wasn't showing off. And perhaps that is the best way of getting children to set standards for themselves, instead of letting them sit back purring smugly over their own achievements.

To encourage at least a degree of self-education, we had the freedom of Papa's bookshelves, and could read anything we liked except for the *Larousse Médical*, which we were absolutely forbidden to look at. For extra precaution it was stored out of reach (so they thought) on top of Papa's bookcase in the study, so that getting at it was a dangerous and hazardous undertaking. And when we did manage to lower it to the floor without a crash, there was always Marie's extra-sensitive radar system to be reckoned with, so that we had to make do with her rare visits to Nice to have her eye attended to. This delectable book was adorned on every page with the most appalling diseases and conditions, and many of them, as an extra bonus, were in colour. I remember gruesome tumours like Californian sunsets, ears that really *looked* like cauliflowers, strawberry noses, some of them devoid of nostrils, Siamese twins glued together at various parts of their anatomy, and one really sickening case of elephantiasis, in which the patient's penis had grown all the way down to his feet so that it looked for all the world like a third leg. And I remember looking at John with my heart all twisted with pity at the thought that, because of his sex, he too, poor boy, might find himself stumping around in this condition one day.

But summer and winter, whether we were going through a period of education or idleness, the afternoons were always free to feed our animals, tend our own gardens and indulge in an occasional spot of grave-digging in the new cemetery which we had laid out under a fig tree for our dead friends, domestic and otherwise. This was tastefully arranged with gravel paths and little tombstones, on the same pattern as the village cemetery where Grandpapa was buried. It contained the remains of a quantity of birds, several large lizards, two cats, a tortoise which Fang had bitten through to the heart during his stay, and a porcupine. And there was *plenty* of room for new candidates.

These activities kept us going until tea-time, after which we retired to the nursery for drawing, painting or reading (for those of us who had sufficiently mastered the art). Marie as usual read Felix the Cat, Nice-Matin and Punch to Anne and Christine, while they messed about with plasticine, or nodded off to sleep on their chairs.

5

SOME TIME BEFORE we left for the Atlantic coast, the little flat
in the old house was let to a couple of English ladies called Hill
and Maxwell who wrote children's books about the local
'peesants', as my mother used to call them. Maxwell wrote the
stories, and Hill drew the pictures. She was tall and silent as a
totem pole, but Maxwell, who had a sweet white lined face,
infinitely old (she must have been about forty at the time), came
to the rescue just about then. She had short stiff grey hair,
sticking out like straw on either side of her cheeks, and a nice
comfortable hump on her back. She asked me to tea under the
fig tree by the *bassin*, and over the bread and butter and cherry
jam, she started to tell me the history of Vence. And it was not
until years later that I realised we were having *lessons*! At the
end of tea I had to go off and write it all down in *English*. This
took some doing as my spelling was entirely phonetic, and all
kinds of other languages from early infancy kept cropping up
when I got stuck, so that my compositions, if they could be
called that, were sprinkled with the odd word in Provençal, or
Malay, or Italian, and sometimes just plain patois. Miss Maxwell
never turned a hair, but simply remarked, 'I think the English

word is probably this, or that,' or whatever it happened to be. And where the story was concerned, she would simply say, 'Actually it was the Saracens who were the pirates, *not* the Knights Templar. *They* were trying to protect the coast, and the ruins up there in the Baous are all that was left after King Philip the Fair razed their fortress to the ground.' And this was more than puzzling. Why, if they were *good*, did the King burn them all alive? Two other Protectors of the City were the Bishops of Vence, St Veran and St Lambert, both of whom, during the processions, were always carried around the town in glass cases (so you could *see* the true bones). Their original medieval silver caskets had been melted down during the Revolution, and nobody from then on knew what had happened to the saints' relics, until the worthy parish priest, browsing through the biography of St Lambert one fine day in 1914, suddenly came across a scribbled note at the end of the tome, mentioning that the holy bones had been tucked away in a small cupboard behind a picture in the church in Vence. All agog with holy excitement the *Curé* rushed to the spot, and there to be sure were the saintly bones patiently waiting to be discovered and reinstated in their rightful places.

St Lambert it seems, was just good and holy without setting the town on fire, producing a creditable number of miracles on his birthday, and the anniversary of his digging-up. St Veran, who was quite another kettle of fish, was made of stern and heroic stuff, and elected 'Protector of the City' during his life-time, a recognition which he well and truly deserved in my opinion. And this is how he got his promotion.

The Wisigoths had invaded Provence once more on one of their periodic foraging expeditions, and set up camp down in the valley by the Loup River. As these barbarians were notorious for their unendearing habits of kidnapping and head-slicing, and spearing of little children on the tops of their swords, the inhabitants of Vence were in a proper taking at the news of their

[31]

approach. The Bishop, admonishing them for their lack of faith, climbed on his mule and set off to beard the pirates in their own camp. When he arrived at dusk, the Chieftain, who had been celebrating for some time with his men, rushed up with fearful imprecations and his sword raised for striking. The Bishop, sliding off his mule, went down on his knees offering the back of his neck for the blow. As the Chieftain brought the blade down, the sword, to his astonishment, flew out of his hand, making straight for an oak tree into which it crashed head first. 'Well,' he said, surprised, 'I'm jiggered,' (or its contemporary equivalent). 'Very well, Bishop, if my sword blooms overnight and is wreathed in flowers by tomorrow morning, I will acknowledge the miracle, and will spare your neck and your whole town as well. And now I'm off to bed.' He roared at his men, 'Let no one touch the sword or the Bishop until further notice.' The holy man, much relieved by this turn of events, proceeded to the oak tree where he went down on his knees and spent the rest of the night in prayer, while all round him snored and belched and grunted in their sleep. And who would blame the poor man if he did by any chance take divine law into his own hands, bending it just a little in the right direction in case the Almighty was busy elsewhere that night? There was, after all, a great deal at stake, not to speak of his own neck, and it simply wasn't worth taking any chances.

At dawn the Wisigoth crawled out of his tent, bleary-eyed and badly hung-over. 'Well, Bishop,' he croaked, 'have you got a miracle for me?'

'Here you are, my lord,' replied the Saint, 'your noble sword has bloomed and blossomed during the night.' And sure enough, entwined around the handle was a pretty pink convolvulus blooming with many a flower. The pirate, overcome with awe, admitted defeat and forthwith withdrew to the coast with his followers, and from there back to his wild and turbulent shores.

And now, June was here again. The nightingale had begun to sing in the cherry tree. Miss Maxwell declared that nobody should be allowed to grow up without having slept at least one night out of doors at that time of year. Mamma had no objection, but there was serious opposition from Marie who said that the humours of the night would seep into our bones and set up malignant rheumatism which we would never shake off again. As an early heatwave made the grasses steam by day and the stars tremble through the heat haze as soon as night set in, her argument didn't hold water and little Miss Maxwell, brave as a lion, carried the day, and sent us scuttling up to the attic to collect hammocks. These she strung up, dangling over our animal cemetery, among the fig-trees, and tucking us up in rugs, left us there to experience our first night out of doors. Listening intently to the noises of the night, we felt so excited we could hardly breathe. The deafening sound of the cicadas gradually died off and the field crickets set up their plaintive dirge. And suddenly, sharp as a knife, came the first notes of the nightingale. He tried out a few trills at first, then, finding his feet, got going in good earnest. On and on he went, gaining confidence every second, changing the odd note here and there, perfecting his theme and settling down to make a night of it. Pungent smells began to rise out of the ground, a field-mouse squeaked, and fireflies flickered in and out among the fig-leaves, taking their time, allegedly searching for a wife, but in no great hurry to find one. From time to time a fig plopped into the *bassin*, or a goldfish leapt at a firefly, while stretching over us the dark blue sky displayed its myriad stars. Squelchy thumb-sucking noises coming from Anne's hammock announced that she had dropped off, but John and I stayed awake a long time, riveted by the revelations of the hot June night.

It was still pitch dark overhead, although a mustard light edged the horizon over the sea, when we were woken up by the hysterical clatter of the birds. This was the first time I realised that they tuned up *before* daybreak, and by the time the sky grew milky they switched off their racket and grew dead quiet. In fact for about fifteen minutes a strange new warmth puffed up all round, and not a sound was heard anywhere. The world seemed wrapped in cotton-wool. Then gradually the air freshened as the sky grew lighter, twigs and leaves began to rustle as insects got on the move, and not till the sun was well up did the birds tune up again, but this time in a quiet and chatty way, as they hopped about their business, cleaning out their nests and bustling around for grubs.

Next day Miss Maxwell listened to our excited comments, but offered none of her own in reply. Although school was over for the time being, her tea-parties, to my joy, continued under the fig-tree.

From where we sat, chewing bread and jam and delicious apple tart, we had a clear view of Queen Jeanne's castle on the south side of the Baou du Malvan. Even though a ruin, it is still to this day the only man-made thing on that completely bare, denuded hill, where only lavender and mountain herbs will grow.

Probably (I say probably, as I am only guessing) built as a kind of Traitors' Tower for Sovereigns and high-ranking nobility convicted of some crime or other in the fourteenth century, its remains still stand there today as bleak and stark and forbidding as they must have been six hundred years ago. I have never met anyone who has visited the ruin. It is said to be the haunt of ghosts and werewolves and mascos, a particularly powerful brand of witches around these parts, and nobody, not even the shepherds, would dream of going near. According to Miss Maxwell, when Robert the Good, King of Provence died, he left the province to his grand-daughter Jeanne in his will, whom he betrothed to the King of Hungary at the age of eight. But Jeanne had other ideas. This didn't suit her at all, and the minute she was old enough, she had her husband strung up outside her bedroom window at the Court of Naples where she was brought up. As this didn't go down too well with her brother-in-law, Louis of Hungary, and as her grandfather died just about this time, Queen Jeanne found it expedient to leave Naples as soon as could be arranged in order to come and claim her inheritance, the Kingdom of Provence. But Louis of Hungary had done his stuff and when she landed she was, with all the pomp and ceremony due to a sovereign, conducted to the grim castle on the Malvan as a prisoner. In my written account of the affair, I had to produce a picture of the castle as I imagined it to be at the time. And to this day I remember the drawing, with the Queen perched on top of the keep weeping bitterly as crows and witches glided all round in the sky, wolves bayed at the moon and werewolves snarled around the walls.

Before she left Naples, her devoted page, Aubépin, had begged to be allowed to go with her, but the jealous courtiers had refused permission. The page, however, faithfully promised to join the Queen at Christmas. Come Yuletide, and the Mistral was moaning and wailing around the battlements as her Chaplain was celebrating midnight mass, and twenty-year-old Queen Jeanne was biting her nails, a sweet tenor voice was heard above the howling of the wind,

> 'Se ma réino plouro
> leu vole ploura. . . .'

it warbled in Provençal. She waited for no more. Recognising Aubépin's dulcet tones, she rushed outside and there he was, battered by the gale and exhausted by the journey, but triumphant. They rushed into each other's arms, and as they embraced, poor Aubépin gasped and crumpled at her feet. A traitor had sprung out of the shadows and plunged his dagger into the poor young man's back. His blood gushed out and spilled all over the white marble forecourt as he expired. The Queen, having apparently expiated her crime, was released soon after.

Thirty years later, come Christmas once more, and having run through another three husbands by then, she returned on a pilgrimage to the castle. And lo and behold, there was a magnificent may tree covered with small red flowers on the spot where the page Aubépin had dropped down dead. They say that ever since that day the may tree has bloomed on Christmas night at Queen Jeanne's castle, but no one so far has been brave enough to go and see for himself. But one thing is certain: from that day to this, the may tree has been called *aubépine* in French.

All through the war I travelled around the Mediterranean Theatre of War with Hill and Maxwell's little books on Vence, until they, along with all my kit, including my most precious possession, *War and Peace* in one volume, disappeared during the Italian campaign. But *that* is another story.

Soon after, we left for St Georges, and were never to see Miss Maxwell again. After her friend's death, she went a little funny in the head, and one day she was found dead, face down in a few inches of water in the source of the Riou stream high up in the Baous.

There was at that time a regular mania for flying, the kind in which you had to lean over the side to see where you were going, counting the steeples as you went to make sure of landing in the right field. Turned into a kind of mystical experience by St Exupéry, that high priest of the air, it became a sort of cult and nobody was immune from the craze, least of all us. We throbbed along enthusiastically and Marie led the dance when Charles Lindbergh crossed the Atlantic in $33\frac{1}{2}$ hours in a 200 horse-power monoplane. She read us the books of St Exupéry, and although it was all way above our heads, enough of the magic, combined with her own suppressed excitement, trickled through to us to make a lasting impression.

Special coats were made for pilots out of leather for keeping out the cold in the windy heights of the sky. Mamma, reacting in her own individualistic manner and never giving a damn for other people's reactions, acquired one of these garments, so sensible as a protection against the icy blasts of the Mistral. Rigged up in this, with the addition of one of her more fetching cloche hats and a stout pair of golfing shoes, she would set out to do her shopping, visit her friends or sort out her lawyer, or the priest, or the mayor. It was she who, after several of these forays, finally persuaded him to institute a car park in the Grand Jardin, where, up till then, long-distance night-driving lorries used to snooze the day away with their engines belching out thick black murderous oil fumes.

Our new English neighbours, Mr and Mrs Hillier, who had built a house next door, were perfect examples of the backbone of England, and therefore never really able to take root abroad, even though they created as perfect an English garden as they could out of their square of cracked, sun-baked clay. There were lawns, rockeries and herbaceous borders, and two of those heavenly cyprus trees which continually crop up in early Italian Renaissance paintings, with very smooth pale grey stems and close-packed greenery pointing up to the sky like minarets. It was a dream of a garden. But the Hilliers were not entirely happy, as the *bonne-à-tout-faire* was unable, try as she might, to produce English puddings, or fruit cake and Victoria sponges, or first-class steak and kidney pie. So a manservant who had been cook in the merchant navy was imported, and did quite well, until unhinged by loneliness. In his misery the poor man first took to the bottle and then to the hills, where he was found three days later, raving under a juniper bush. But throughout all these vicissitudes, Mrs H. remained calm and unperturbed. She produced a baby girl, for whom she made a delightful chintzy nursery, then she got down to the Victoria sponges herself. I loved helping her in the kitchen, and watching her bath and feed the baby in that bright, gay nursery, so unlike our own, with the photographs of Marie's dead husband and baby glooming over us day and night.

These frequent visits to Mrs Hillier's kitchen and nursery helped to keep my English going, which, since our return from Malaya, would have completely withered otherwise.

In another effort to keep up our English, Mamma took us to an English children's 'club' run in the village by 'Auntie', on the first floor of her tea-room on the Place Peyra. This is now called the *Pigeonnier* and is still run as a tea-room, but no longer alas by Auntie. There we played Happy Families, Hunt the Slipper, Postman's Knock and Hide and Seek.

'Auntie' was a middle-aged English spinster, who had lived in Vence from time immemorial, and who befriended painters and writers. Norman Douglas always stayed with her on his way through (presumably to and from Capri), and after D. H. Lawrence had come to die at the Villa Keja next door to the Mas Mistral, Auntie rooted out his gravestone and stored it under her kitchen sink for safe keeping. It was always fascinating to slip away from Happy Families upstairs and sneak into the tea-room on the ground floor to listen to the grown-ups' chatter. Auntie, who always insisted on speaking her atrocious French to my mother (who invariably answered in her equally atrocious English—but as neither listened to the other, it did not matter in the slightest, and everybody was perfectly happy), returned from Nice one day after an appendix operation, firmly convinced that a pair of forceps had been left inside her. She could feel them rattling, she declared, as she shuffled around her tea-room. And insisting on being opened up again, she was proved right, and the instrument which she proudly kept under a glass dome, was always produced for her guests' inspection. Vegetarians and nudists ('cranks', as we called them) frequently dropped in for tea and toasted buns, and we sometimes came across their camps during our country walks. Given to beards and sandals and fringy garments (when they wore anything at all) they were the forerunners of today's hippy communities. One of them, 'Jesus Christ', was a great favourite of ours. Gentle and harmless, he drifted about the streets in long flowing robes, with curly hair and beard, looking noble and prophetic, a character straight out of the Bible.

One person we dreaded, however, was the *Folle du Sacré-Coeur*, whose house nestled at the foot of the railway bridge, shaded by palms and banana trees. Day in, day out, winter and summer, she stood on the bridge by the gate, clad in a dressing-gown with a feather boa round her neck, catching people as they passed. If you prudently walked on the other side, hoping to slip by unnoticed and pretending not to see her, she shouted for you to come across, then insults and *grossièretés* followed, while you scuttled on as fast as you could, blushing with shame and embarrassment. There was also a red-headed female who patrolled the streets all day and petrified my father. She would come sliding up to him in the street, ask the time of day, and upon being told, crowed like a cock before tripping off towards her next victim.

We often met Gordon Craig, swinging along in his black cloak and hat, and he and Papa politely bowed to each other, while a civil exchange of 'morning Craig, morning Fesq' passed between them. But as far as I know, the friendship went no further.

Matisse, who lived on the route de St Jeannet, hardly ever left his house, whereas Chagall was often seen, prowling around the market stalls.

Another character who also flourished at that time and floundered about the streets of Vence carting buckets of raw, bleeding meat, was a wild-looking woman who inhabited a large house at L'Ara, in which she harboured five or six dozen cats. Her downtrodden husband was miserably eking out the last days of his life under the same roof in total neglect. His wife and her trusty serving wench crouched all day long over the kitchen fire with a bottle of wine between them, while the cats spat and hissed at one another over the buckets of meat, and the wretched husband lay dying in his soiled, unchanged sheets. The cats, which he feared and hated, spent long busy nights with him, conducting passionate love affairs, fighting one another to the death, and leaving their messes all over his bed. At the end of the war when, after a long and protracted agony, the poor man was eventually sped on his way out of this world with the cats' assistance, his wife packed up all their mutual belongings and trundled them up to the Mas Mistral, to be stored in the attic for safe-keeping. Why my mother, in the unthinking kindness of her heart, permitted such a performance to take place under her roof, is hard to tell, but Anne's husband, who was there at the time and was press-ganged willy-nilly into helping with the operation, told me recently that even the largest pieces of furniture were heaved up the attic stairs.

The poor woman was eventually taken off to an asylum when her behaviour, even by Vence standards, became too eccentric. I often passed her sitting on a stone at her garden gate, upbraiding her geraniums in accusing and reproachful tones.

6

I THINK OUR impending confirmation was the reason for the priest's presence at lunch that day. Mamma, who was on good terms with the Church on the whole, only occasionally telling the priest how to run his affairs (which he always took very well) didn't, however, encourage the clergy beyond reason. They were all right in their place but no further, as indeed we were to find out at that fateful lunch. Now that the boot was on the other foot, the priest was going to have his own back.

'Well, my girl,' he said, turning to me, 'and what class are you in now?'

'We don't have classes,' I explained, 'we used to have lessons. Now we don't have anything. It's a kind of holiday.'

'Indeed,' said the priest with interest, 'other children aren't on holiday at the moment, as far as I know!' (Little indeed *did* he know!)

'Their governess left a few weeks ago, and I haven't been able to find them another one yet,' said Mamma placidly. 'Do have a little more stew, *Curé*,' she added, eyeing his hollow cheeks and stringy neck. Everybody knew that parish priests invariably lived on the breadline.

He gratefully held out his plate and returned to the subject in hand.

'But why do they need a governess?' he asked, surprised.

'Well,' said Mamma reasonably, 'they have to have *some* sort of education. Mind you, they can read and write,' she added hastily.

'But why don't they go to school?' asked the priest, frankly puzzled.

'School? What School? We tried Sévigné, but somehow it didn't seem to work, and there isn't another one in Vence.'

'What about the village school? What's wrong with that?'

'The *village* school?' Mamma looked startled. That was *one* thing she hadn't thought of. Why indeed *not* the village school? Always open-minded, she was quite prepared to consider this new idea.

Inwardly I cursed this priestly interference. Why didn't he mind his own business and stick to confirmation and confession, quite bad enough, anyway, without having to step outside his own province? I had always considered our priest a good and harmless man, feeling quite neutral towards him, if anything even a little on the friendly side, but why in the name of heaven didn't he stick to his own business? Life was difficult enough with governesses, but if now *school* was to be introduced, it would become quite unmanageable.

And so it came to pass that we were enrolled at the village school after the summer holidays.

On the first day of term Mamma, determined to do the thing properly now that she was launched, took a long, searching look at the other children to see how they were turned out. And so a few days later we were rigged out as little peasants with wooden-soled lace-up boots and rough-haired navy cloaks reaching down to the ankle. This bulky garment, so useful to shepherds high up in the icy mountain passes of the Baous, was much too hot and heavy on balmy autumn days, and quite intractable in a raging wind, when the Mistral, roaring down the railway cutting, would lift it high in the air as you struggled across the bridge, then smash it down over your head, knocking you off your feet at the same time.

School was in fact not as bad as we had expected. We were forty strong in the classroom and the windows were nailed down for the winter. The coal stove, red-hot and roaring steadily, belched out its deadly fumes all day long. On wet days there was a stifling smell of steaming child in the air. Those who had been sewn into their clothes for the winter itched and scratched a good deal as the heat of the room increased, and the heavy winter bouquet of the classroom must have been a sore trial to the teacher.

After paying deliberate attention to fractions, parsing, algebra and various other incomprehensible subjects which might just as well have been in Chinese, I decided to ignore their existence and concentrate on French literature and natural history, this last subject being deplorably elementary. Thanks to Marie, I seemed to know quite a bit more than they were trying to teach us.

To begin with, following Mamma's decision that we would conform in every way, we had lunch in the canteen where the only course, soup, was served in army mess tins, together with half a loaf of bread. The boys, whose school was on the other side of the playground wall, joined us for this feast, but we were forbidden to talk to one another. John, whenever I caught sight of him, looked so glum that it made me want to cry, but Anne seemed to have found her feet and was always the animated centre of a fascinated group obviously hanging on her words. I often wondered what stories she was telling them.

Goodness knows what went wrong with this arrangement, but it soon came to an end. We were thereafter provided with a packet of sandwiches each before leaving the house at seven-thirty in the morning. As we were forbidden to stay in the classroom during the lunch hour or to sit in the canteen with our superior sandwiches, we huddled together in the cold, dusty windswept school yard, disconsolately munching our roast beef sandwiches and apple tart, or whatever other delicacy was on the menu for the day.

Again, I am perfectly certain that none of us complained, as we were quite used to taking things in our stride, philosophically accepting discomfort, and heartily enjoying the goodies when they came our way. But this period came to an end, quite abruptly, and, most blissful of all, suddenly we didn't have to go to school any more. As these decisions were taken behind our backs we never knew the reason for life, all of a sudden, going into such happy reverse.

The spring was there again, and we moved back to the Mistral. Intoxicated with our new freedom, we galloped up and down the garden, yelling our lungs out to let off steam, rolling down the sloping banks and pelting all the way downhill to the bottom field. After a couple of days we sobered down and returned to our private occupations which had been so boringly interrupted by school.

The animal cemetery had been badly neglected. The paths needed weeding, some of the crosses had fallen flat on their faces, and a quail's sepulchre had been desecrated by a cat. When all this was cleared and tidied up, I went to inspect my own garden behind the mimosa trees. Here all was desolation and decay. The soil was dry and cracked like flaking scabs, and all my plants had died from lack of water and loving care. The giant thistle which I had carefully dug up on one of our walks and transplanted into my herbaceous border, had frizzled up beyond reclaim; my best clump of dandelions was drooping sadly, the marigolds were smothered with blackfly, and my fragile ragged robin, so difficult to rear since the beginning, in spite of the stewed prunes which I had saved up from lunch and forked into its roots to feed them up, had swooned and melted right away. Totally discouraged, I went off to check up on what was going on in the hedge which grew along the eastern boundary of the garden, where oaks, hazel and fig-trees flourished undisturbed, with here and there a few clumps of bamboo canes to break up the monotony. In the spring and early summer a nightingale spent his nights and days singing his little heart out. Blackbirds, blue tits and finches ran up their annual nests there, and tree-creepers and woodpeckers had their permanent holes.

A pair of jays flapped around making a great deal of fuss for many years, and cuckoos were all around, popping their eggs into other people's baskets. It was pure bliss lying in the grass absolutely still, watching the busy life of the hedge in daily progress. The fig-trees were swarming with herds of little dome-shaped grey bugs which looked like minute elephants, with crispy hides which cracked like egg-shell under pressure. The birds were very partial to these, popping over to the fig-trees for a quick peck or two among the herds whenever they had a minute to spare. Ants kept flocks of a curious little flea-like animal perched on tall, delicate, hair-like legs which got hopelessly tangled up when they were being briskly hustled along to fresh pastures by the ants. Lizards, lying in wait would mop up whole flocks in one sitting, gobbling up the sheep and the shepherds indiscriminately. On the ground among last year's dead leaves quite another kind of activity existed, and a very different way of life was carried on with single-minded dedication and great purposefulness. It was the feeling of total certainty oozing from these creatures, that they were doing the right thing at all times, which continually astonished me. Doubt never seemed to enter their tiny minds as they carried on with dogged perseverence, like the ant towing a grasshopper's wing all the way up one side of a blade of grass, then down the other, on its way to the family nest.

Another creature on whose habits I could have improved if asked for my advice was a plump white grub which persisted in travelling on its back, waving its legs in the air, scudding along the ground at breakneck speed by a series of twists and wriggles and contortions, all hopelessly inefficient and only too obviously uncomfortable. No matter how often I set him on his feet, over he would go, *throwing* himself on his back again. This was simply asking for trouble, and it wasn't long before he got it. Along came a great big hornet who, spying the foolish creature displaying its soft and juicy under-parts, landed square on its belly. This threw the maggot into a frenzy of wriggles, racing along faster than ever, with the hornet riding him like a horse. After a minute or two of this useless activity, the grub tried to unseat his rider by curling himself up, thereby offering the hornet just the spot he was looking for, and into which he promptly plunged his dagger. The grub flopped at once and went quite limp, so that I thought all was over and done with. But nothing of the kind. The brute now settled himself comfortably, wriggling the sting about in the wound, presumably squirting poison into the various vital organs. When remembering the last hornet sting I had suffered, my heart went out to the poor little beast whose eyes were popping out of its head, and whose whiskers waggled frantically in all directions. The hornet suddenly stopped dead and a look of intense concentration came over its face. Quite exhausted, I thought, having a little rest before he pulls the thing out. And it was not till years later that I discovered what was going on. The hornet, having at last found her goal, was actually, at this precise moment laying her eggs in the wretched maggot's solar plexus. I ask you!

7

ONE FINE SPRING afternoon Mrs Hillier came to tea, and to
our surprise, although we were playing quite noisily just outside
the drawing-room windows, we were not asked to come in and
pay our respects. After about an hour of earnest confabulation,
Mrs Hillier appeared on the doorstep. We ran up to say hullo
for manners' sake. Our neighbour was saying, 'So you see, my
dear, we must stick together.'

'Of course,' agreed Mamma fervently, 'I quite agree with
you.'

'If it weren't for the baby,' added Mrs Hillier, 'I would go
myself, but I can't really leave her at the moment.'

'Don't worry,' said my mother, 'I will go tomorrow, and the
children will come with me.' This sounded promising. Where
were we going tomorrow, we wanted to know? After Mrs
Hillier had gone we were informed of the treat in store. A
family of Poor Whites had apparently come to settle in Vence,
and were squatting, in utter penury, in a deserted farmhouse at
La Sine. It was generally believed that they came from Ireland,
that the husband was an alcoholic, and that the numerous
children ran about barefoot and unfed, as the family was totally

destitute. Mrs Hillier, having had wind of the affair, and not wanting to get mixed up herself, had approached my mother, knowing she wouldn't be turned down. Turned down indeed! Mamma, throwing herself into the venture full-tilt, made us bring our rucksacks and filled them to the brim with all the preserves she could lay her hands on. Jams, pickled goose, carefully saved up by Madame Rose for winter cassoulets, homemade chicken liver pâtés, quails preserved in brandy sauce, and all kinds of salted vegetables and sugared fruit. Also the last pot of honey from our own hives, whose loss I at least welcomed as good riddance.

Next morning, booted as for mountaineering, we harnessed ourselves to our rucksacks, picked up a stout walking stick each and set off down the hill, plodding across the valley in single file to La Sine.

We forded the little stream of the Malvan in full spate and trudged on until we reached the clearing which Mrs Hillier had described. And there, indeed, stood the old farmhouse with its tiny windows like half-closed eyes, rather *dégringolé* about the roof and top floor, but nevertheless adequate enough to house a large family of Poor Whites.

A huge chestnut tree spread its branches over the roof, and all round grew the finest, shortest emerald green grass I had ever seen. It could have been a well cared-for bowling-green. Surrounding this unbelievably beautiful fairy-tale spot were olive groves, cypresses and orange trees, and no sign of any other habitation as far as you could see. Lying all round the house were empty tins, beer bottles, and hundreds, literally *hundreds* of empty wine bottles. As we approached a dog barked and a flock of small children poured out of the front door, followed by the mother herself. She stared at us in silence as Mamma explained the purpose of our visit, and moved nearer to the front door. The dog, snarling, barred the way. We didn't appear to be very welcome. As the woman continued to glare, without a word,

Mamma, not in the least disconcerted, said, 'I expect the lady is busy. She wasn't expecting us. Unpack your bags, children, and put the stuff on the grass.'

While we did as we were bid, I took a quick look round at the children, a scruffy unruly mob who were milling about with excited squeaks, picking things up and running to their mother, screeching in an unknown language with vaguely English-sounding vowels. Monolithic and silent, the woman continued to stare until we had deposited the last pot on the grass. Then, in icy tones, she asked, 'And to whom, may I ask, do I owe this bounty?'

'I am Mrs Fesq,' chirruped Mamma, not in the least put out by the frigidity of the reception. 'And these are my children. You are Mrs O'Connor, I believe?'

'That is correct,' snapped the woman.

'What a lovely family you have,' prattled Mamma, lying in her teeth, as the grubby-looking brood continued to mill around noisily. At that moment a large and lumpy girl, very much bigger and at least two years older than myself came out of the house.

'This is my step-daughter,' said Mrs O'Connor, mentioning no names and giving away as little as she could. The girl stared in silence as Mrs O'Connor had done.

On the way home, relieved of our loads and a curiously un-rewarding experience, we skipped along merrily, picking wild flowers and peering into the bushes for birds' nests, assuming this to be the end of the Poor Whites as far as we were con-cerned. But we still, after all these years, didn't know our mother.

'What a charming family,' said Mamma, as I was extricating Anne from a bog into which she had sunk up to her knees. 'We must have them round to tea and you will look after the child-ren, won't you,' she said, tapping me lightly on the head with a hazel twig. My heart sank into my mountain boots, but too well drilled by Marie's iron discipline to argue, I took this in silence, all joy frizzled away at one stroke for the rest of the walk.

When it came to the point, the small rabble, thank God, had been left behind and the only one I had to deal with was the lumpy girl. John and Anne, needless to say, had vanished off the face of the earth, so I took her upstairs to my room and introduced her to my doll, Genitalia. The girl, whose name I still didn't know, stared in bored silence.

'Would you like to see my books?' I tried next, and then suddenly a thought struck me, 'you *can* read, can't you?' I asked tactlessly. She gave me a withering look, but forbore to answer. Oh God, I thought, now I've put my foot in it. She's in a huff. Completely at a loss to know what to do with this unresponsive creature, I thought I'd better take matters in hand and ask no more questions.

'Come,' I said, firmly, 'we'll take a walk around the garden.' I showed her the animal cemetery, the goldfish in the *bassin*, the strawberry beds, by which time we had reached the top of the garden, with me conducting a running commentary on points of interest as we came across them.

'And here, the donkeys from next door come through a hole in the fence to eat our raspberries,' and 'if you look up in that tree you will see the jays' nest.' Further up there was an anthill, where your toes would be chewed off to the bone in a matter of minutes if you stepped on it, and a little way on, a viper's nest heaving with black worm-like babies. At the sight of these she sprang back as if she'd been bitten and gave me a stern look of reproof, but still didn't open her mouth.

By the time we got to the top of the garden, I was at my wits' end. This is my last effort I thought, after that she can go to hell, and offering her the freedom of my favourite climbing tree, and the ultimate in hospitality, I said, 'If you care to climb to the top, you get a first-class view of people dying in their beds on the balconies over there,' and I pointed out the vast TB hospital adjoining our garden, where the poor patients, lying in the blazing sun as was then the fashion, were coughing their lungs out and rendering up the ghost at the rate of two or three a day.

After that, I am glad to say, there were no more visitations from the Poor Whites.

8

IT WAS NOT until three years later, when I was thirteen, that, as June drew to an end and summer was heating up, Mamma felt the call of the Atlantic beating in her veins again. A villa was booked in St Georges, and once more the leather trunks came thumping down the attic stairs, propelled by Rubio's rope-soled *espadrilles*. The thought of another long hot summer holiday in St Georges sent us reeling drunkenly about the garden in a state of rapturous excitement. Papa, who was due for leave again, would meet us at the station in Marseilles, and we would continue on the journey together.

It was so long since we had seen him that he looked unfamiliar, and if he was pleased to see us, he showed no sign of it. Apart from deep and frequent sighs, tapping his breast as if in pain and rolling his eyes up to the ceiling, he appeared in good spirits, and although he ignored us throughout the entire journey, only addressing a few words in German to Marie, it was a great joy to see him again, and to know that we would have him with us for three whole months. Everything went well, the midnight feast which Marie produced was up to its usual standard, nobody was sick, or got trapped in the *toilettes*, and the train arrived on time. There were plenty of taxis at the station when we arrived (the horse carriages, no longer on station duty, plied their trade up and down the sea-front for the benefit of tourists).

Although just as uncomfortable as we expected, 'Pépé' was one of the least smelly of our summer villas. A paved, walled yard at the back contained a companionable two-seater privy, with little round windows cut in the door for callers to peer in and see who was at home.

Marie, who was once more doing the cooking, had to sweat over the usual furnace to make the merest cup of tea, and the whole house was shrouded in the dust of the preceding winter. We all managed to fit in somehow; which was an achievement, as the house was much smaller than anything we had lived in so far. Rubio was squeezed into a kitchen cupboard, and Anne, Christine and I crammed ourselves into a tiny bedroom; John moved in with Marie, and my parents got a room to themselves. Sam, the cocker spaniel, snorted and whimpered the night away in the dining-room.

The discomfort of the house worried us children very little, as we spent all our time on the beach, or at Nostram with the Darlanges. As long as we turned up for meals, we had the most complete and blessed freedom. Always, of course, excepting the morning, when we had to resume our gym lessons with M. Coulon. And so the swimming lessons started up again (tacked onto the end of the daily gym class), and dragged on and on, throughout our precious holiday, until finally M. Coulon declared that we were fit to take the test. This included life-saving as well, for good measure.

The ordeal took place in the harbour, in front of the entire village assembled on the beach and along the jetty, where the fire brigade's brass band was blaring rousing marches. The judges sat in a rowing-boat at the end of our 'run', where we had to turn and go back to the starting point.

There had been a heavy storm the day before, and the sea was dark and murky. When we lined up at the starting point on the pier and looked down, we saw that the water was bubbling with jellyfish. With a gasp of horror I turned to M. Coulon, and said that we couldn't possibly swim in THAT! His only answer was to push me in. We all flopped on top of the soft yielding mush, and went under, and thrashed about among the jellyfish. It was like trying to swim in tapioca pudding. Within seconds, their tentacles were twined around my arms, creeping round my neck and trailing across my face. Somehow or other, most of us managed to struggle to the boat (though some of the children went under and had to be hooked out, as they showed no sign of reappearing), then started back on the return journey. As we tried to scramble back onto the jetty, we were pushed in again to do the life-saving bit, and had in turn to drag someone as far as the judges' boat once more, and then be dragged ourselves. As my own dragger was in an even worse state of panic than I was, she pulled me under much more than above the water. When at last I reached dry land, my mouth, full of jellyfish, felt as if I had chewed a hornets' nest.

The ordeal was over, but we were covered with stinging weals on every inch of uncovered skin. By the evening, we were puffed up all over as if blown up with a bicycle pump, and our swollen eyelids were glued together. Marie, grinding her false teeth with disapproval, dumped us into a bath of boracic water, and spent the next few hours sponging our throbbing faces.

When we could swim tolerably well, Mamma, ever pursuing her aim of trying to improve our physique, devised a most terrible, lolloping walk for us, which was designed to arch the feet, loosen up the joints and tone the muscles all in one go. It was, according to her, the best possible exercise for developing young growing bodies, so two or three times a week, we were marched off to the pine woods along the beach, thereby getting double benefit from the performance, as we would be breathing in all those valuable essences at the same time.

Completely unselfconscious as she was, she broke into her lollop, enjoining us to do the same, before we had even left the village. John and Anne followed her, doubled-up with giggles, while I hobbled behind, with tears of shame and humiliation running down my face, as people stopped, stared, and exclaimed 'Oh, poor things, do look! Whatever is the matter with them?' We looked like a family of spastics all cursed with the same affliction. Curiously, Mamma minded the giggles much less than the tears, which she said I produced on purpose to draw attention to myself and make people feel sorry for me. And so we lolloped along, rocking from heel to toe, flexing the knees, flinging out the arms ('from the *shoulder*, I tell you! Those feeble little wiggles are no good at all!') and thrusting out the hip joints this way and that like a school of belly dancers. When this performance was over, and we had hobbled disjointedly back to Pépé, we rushed off to the beach as fast as we could, in case Mamma should think up some new form of body-building exercise for us.

It was a great joy to be able to swim. No breaker, however large, was frightening any longer. We dived straight into it, gliding through the glassy water, and learnt, by using our legs as rudders, how far we could go before surfacing again. A wooden construction, like a scaffold planted in the sand, served as a diving board when the tide was in. An ordinary raft was out of the question, as it would have been dragged out, anchors and all, by the powerful sucking action of the retreating tide. When the sea went out so far, it had a kind of indecent look, like people who show too much gum when they smile.

Twice a year when this happened at the time of the Equinox, the harbour was drained to the dregs, exposing to view all the treasures of its bottom; old prams, cartwheels, toy boats, fragments of bidets and so on. The firm wet sand-line came to an abrupt end and the primeval oceanic ooze stretched out for miles ahead, bubbling and wriggling with its own private life. Lugworm, like strips of raw liver, dived head down into the slime, razor shells peered out of their holes, little green crabs, terrified of being frizzled up by the sun or picked off by seagulls scrambled frantically into the mud, and all kinds of nameless, shapeless blobs of jelly wriggled and twisted about, impatiently waiting for the sea to return. And all this snapped, crackled and popped as millions of tiny bubbles continually burst everywhere for miles around. The first time we witnessed this phenomenon, we ran excitedly along the edge, breathing in the deep and satisfyingly rich smell which came wafting out of the ooze. Suddenly, overpowered by an irresistible urge, I threw myself flat on my face on the mud. The other two followed instantly, and we rolled about, slapping and whacking the gluey stuff with flaying arms, unconsciously reaching back millions of years to our original home in the warm, soupy Cambrian seas where our ancestors, those bits of quivering jelly, first came to life. Black from head to foot, we jumped back on to the solid sand and raced home to show ourselves to Marie who, we felt, would surely be fascinated by the look and feel of this extraordinary mud so seldom seen. Instinct warned us to avoid the front door. We trooped into the kitchen where Marie, with spectacles all steamed up, was waging her daily battle with the furnace. Watching our approach without turning a hair she simply said, 'Stay on the doorstep, I don't want you dripping all over my floor.'

'What do you think of this, Marie?' asked John, 'have you ever seen anything like it before?' She ran a finger down his arm and rubbed it on the palm of her other hand thoughtfully. 'Good rich stuff this, very fertile. There's nothing to beat it. I'll get Rubio to fetch a few pails of it for the garden,' she said. Suddenly there was a roar from the dining-room.

'Good God, what is this terrible pong?' It was a voice we knew well, issuing from the Colonel's wife, who prided herself on always speaking her mind. We had forgotten that Mamma was holding one of her terrible tea-parties that day.

'Is there anything the matter with your drains?' queried another voice.

'It smells more like a dead rat under the floorboards to me,' contributed a third.

'Marie,' squeaked Mamma in a quavering voice, 'what is that appalling stench?'

At this point Anne, always the bravest of us all, darted across the kitchen, and poked her black face round the door, flashing her buck teeth at them in an engaging grin. A gasp of horror arose from the startled ladies. At the same instant Sam, who had been snoozing at Mamma's feet patiently waiting for crumbs from the rich man's table, was suddenly brought back to life by the intriguing odour. With a joyful bark he leapt forward, catching one of his toenails in the lace edge of the table-cloth. There was a resounding crash, and Anne shot back into the kitchen, banging the door. Marie pushed us all out to the yard, hissing fiercely, 'Get back to the beach at once and wash all that filth off in the sea. And don't let me see you again before dinner.'

When the tide was rising, ah, that was when our spirits soared, and a strange, inexplicable elation took possession of us all. This reaction to the advancing tide was not confined to us alone, as quite a detectable feeling of excitement rippled along the beach like an electric current. And the higher the tide rose, the more delighted we all were. On very special occasions, freak waves even swamped the tents and carried away bits of underwear, parasols, canvas shoes and all sorts of other treasures, and we dived in like retrievers, to restore their sodden property to the distracted owners. It was then that the *plongeoir* (the diving contraption) came into its own, and we all swam out and scrambled up the slippery wooden scaffolding to the top, dived in and climbed up again. It was enormous fun swimming all round under water among the shoals of small fish which clustered around. Completely unafraid, they escorted us, swimming in and out of our hair, wriggling through our fingers and peering into our ears.

This swimming and diving and playing around with the fish was so absorbing, that we were sometimes caught unawares, and left high and dry by the retreating tide. One day when this had happened, and we were diving from the top of the *plongeoir* into very shallow water, I landed straight on my head on the sandy bottom. Had it been stones I would have broken my neck, instead of which my backbone merely slipped out of joint. But even this was bad enough to keep me flat on my back for the rest of the summer. Plunged into despair, I think I would have died of boredom and frustration, had Jacques not come every day to sit by my bed for hours, reading aloud, playing rummy, the hanging corpse and the battle-ship game. He came straight from the beach, smelling of seaweed and dripping sand everywhere. My gratitude for all those hours of swimming ungrudgingly sacrificed, to sit with me and keep up my morale, was unbounded, and my devotion and admiration for him grew as the days went by, and he still came, patient and forbearing, while the others simply put their heads round the door to say hullo, and were gone. So that by the end of the summer, I was totally, unquestioningly, in love with him, as a dog is in love with his master.

Towards the middle of September I was allowed to sit up in bed for a few days, and then to stand up and come downstairs. But there was no more swimming that year.

At about this time my mother had another of her fiendish inspirations which could turn one day after another into a ghastly nightmare, when the high tides of the autumn Equinox revealed, upon retiring miles out in the bay, the largest oyster beds imaginable, clinging to a vast shelf of rock, usually hidden by the sea. Mamma spotted these oyster beds at once, and day after day during the *grandes marais* she sent Rubio hotfoot with a sack and hammer and chisel, to collect as many as he could, before the tide returned and swept him out to sea. So for days and days he came home with his sack heavily loaded with huge oysters as large as Marie's gardening shoes. Now I know that anybody in their senses would have been delighted at the prospect of these daily feasts. But unfortunately for me I was, as so often, out of my senses, and the mere sight of these obscene creatures, glistening in their shells on my plate, made my insides heave. If I could manage to get the first one down, all was well, and I bolted the rest with my eyes closed. But more often than not, merely sticking a fork into them made them writhe and squirm so much that I usually had to rush out of the room with my napkin over my face. When I managed to stick it out, it was a matter of twining the brute around the fork and pulling as hard as I could, for it clung to its shell with amazing tenacity. John and Anne scooped theirs out with the greatest of ease, and a smug expression on their faces. They positively *enjoyed* eating oysters, whereas for me, the whole process was barbaric and revolting. My mother's neck used to go puce with anger at my panic and horror. She could not understand why I made such a fuss, and called me a *petite nature* (in her eyes the most contemptible thing anybody could ever be) and the meal usually ended with me rushing out of the room howling, 'You don't realise, they've even got *kidneys*!'

That summer, we developed a mania for seine fishing. John and Jacques would wade out up to their armpits dragging the enormous thirty yard long net, while we, the girls, hung on to the other end, stumbling about in the water under the weight, and being sworn at by the boys. After floundering along for half a mile or so they would struggle out of the water, towing the heavily-laden net on to the firm damp sand. By then, it was heaving and wriggling with all its captives writhing and leaping in wild panic. Most of the catch, consisting of jellyfish, had to be thrown out. The graceful little seahorses we carried carefully back to the water, as well as the squids and all their cousins and their sisters and their aunts. But fish of every kind, crabs, clams and scallops we popped into buckets of sea-water to be turned into delicious dinners. Sam, who followed the net from the shore and helped sort out the catch, would often be turned into the catch himself, when he officiously poked his nose into the net and came out squealing with a crab firmly fixed on to the end of it. But he never seemed to learn and whenever he came across a pool at low tide, in he waded up to his ears, always mortally offended whenever he came to grief.

That summer, out of the blue, Mamma took me to Barbezieux, to stay with her friends the Fauconniers. Hélène was there with her three brothers, all of them cool, detached and haughty like highly-bred hawks. François Fontaine was there also, who was later to become Hélène's husband. *He* was less of a bird of prey than a stag, and God knows how *I* looked to them! Anyway, after a while the ice melted, and we all played noisy and rumbustious games in the garden. There were swings and a trapeze and parallel bars, and that peculiar overriding melancholy which broods over the region around Bordeaux and which pervades all the novels of Mauriac. Insidious and seductive like a kind of lotus eating, I felt even then that it could, if allowed, soak into the bloodstream and fix in it a permanent mood of languid melancholy for life. More than ever did I sympathise with those full-blooded adventurous pioneers, my two great grandfathers, for getting away from this cloying, dreamy, enervating miasma.

Henri Fauconnier's sister, Geneviève, who wrote that blissful book about her farm, *Pastorale*, and got the Prix Femina for her novel *Claude*, lived a long way out in the country. Thither we all repaired one fine day, and *there* was a scene straight out of Alain Fournier's book *Le Grand Meaulnes*. The farm and its grounds had been given over for the day to some charity or other, and there were booths, merry-go-rounds and coconut shies everywhere. Children in crinolines and knickerbockers raced around with hoops along the paths, laughing and shouting.

We then went into a barn, smelling of warm cow and hay and there, of all unexpected things, two American ladies who lived in a caravan in the grounds, danced a ballet to Debussy's *L'Après-midi d'un Faune*. The whole thing in my memory is so nebulous and dreamlike that, much as I would like to, I can't remember anything more precise .There was a great deal of old world courtesy around and Mamma was continuously having her hand kissed, which she didn't seem to mind in the least.

John, on the whole, was a calm and placid person, wise beyond his years, and when people approached him about their problems, as they often did, his advice was always judicious and succinct. But once in a while the Devil pulled off a tremendous coup and got into him. And when that happened, he became a *Gnat*, and the only thing to do was to keep as far away from him as possible. On that fateful day when Rubio tried to kill him, we had all gone off to the forest to collect wood for Marie's furnace. Rubio, armed with a hatchet, was harnessed to a little two-wheeler trailer, and we each had our rucksacks on our backs. The weather was lovely and we skipped along in high spirits. Even Sam, who was beginning to show his age, trotted briskly along the sandy path, displaying an unusual crispness of manner. When we reached the spot we had in mind, where we knew a lot of dead trees were hanging around waiting for the chop, Rubio got to work with his axe, and we helped by pulling off the prickly branches and breaking them up into suitable lengths.

We had been at work for about half an hour or so when, with a sinking heart, I noticed John's mood changing. He was beginning to snap his sticks with exaggerated effort, flinging his arms out in a wide gesture so that one of us got scratched across the face or poked in the eye every time. When he caught Anne's skirt, lifting it high up on the end of a twig, and roared with laughter, she whipped round in a fury. 'I'll hit you with my teeth if you're not careful,' she snarled. Rubio, coming in for the next round, got a sharp sting on the back of the neck. He missed a stroke and went sprawling past his target, landing on his knees with his beret over his nose. Again John hooted at the sight. Rubio's fierce Basque temper was roused, he scrambled to his feet with a growl of rage and made straight for John with his chopper raised above his head. I yelled, 'Run, run, for God's sake! RUN!'

John, leaping like a goat, bolted through the trees with an infuriated Rubio staggering after him. But owing to his weak sight (his eyeballs had been badly scorched in a thunderstorm by a particularly vicious flash of lightning) he kept stumbling over stones and stumps which he couldn't see, and John got away. But after that episode, and although we all begged and pleaded for his reprieve, poor Rubio was sent back to the Mas Mistral in disgrace and we never saw him again.

9

MAMMA, UPON WHOM was vouchsafed another flash from On High, announced one day that we would not be returning to Vence for the winter, that she was going back to Malaya, and would take us all with her. We whooped and danced with joy at this, but the next day, having changed her mind, she bustled off to see the headmaster of the Collège de Royan about our confounded education. It transpired from this interview that he would take us all, on condition that *I* should learn Latin before the beginning of term. (There were about two weeks to go.) Mamma confidently assured him that there was no problem, and set out at once to find me a Latin master. This turned out to be more difficult than she anticipated. The priest, who should have been a natural, flatly refused to teach girls. All the teachers were still away on holiday, but finally she unearthed a very ancient scholar, who was spending the remainder of his days writing the history of medieval heresies in Latin.

Not knowing what I was in for, and, enchanted at having to learn such a noble and ancient language (Sanskrit would have been even better) I plunged into it with great enthusiasm, although I must admit I got a shock when my new teacher

[63]

greeted me in Latin on arrival, and never addressed a word to me in any other language during the entire period of our association. For six hours a day from then on we were incarcerated together in his study, while my poor untutored brain reeled in complete bewilderment, until the evening, when I staggered down to the beach completely bemused, for a quick swim, before creeping back to my room to my Latin homework. Never had I worked so hard in my life.

When school started, we did not, thank goodness, have to take an entrance examination—that would have been disastrous. A rough guess was made, and we were placed in classes suited to our respective ages, if not to our intellectual capacity. As it turned out, once installed in our classrooms, we managed, by dint of a great deal of hard work, and a certain amount of copying from our neighbours, to scrape along with the dunces at the bottom of the class. Our delight at being in a proper school, with mature, grown-up children of our own age, kept our spirits up, so that our low marks and total incomprehension of some of the subjects did not really depress us *too* much. Among the subjects which we enjoyed were ancient history, plain straightforward English which presented no problem, and biology, which taught us some fascinating facts. We learnt, for instance, that the human eyelid possesses the only muscle in the body which makes a noise: if you bang your eye shut, you can hear a little click, But you have to listen carefully, as it is a very *small* click.

By saving up my pocket money for several weeks, I was able to buy a magnifying glass, and settle down to the study of the insect population of the garden. Spiders, which far outnumbered everything else, were sensitive to noise, as I discovered by creeping up behind them and suddenly shouting 'boo'. All their legs stretched out with fright, so that they lost hold and fell out of their webs, unwinding their lifeline as they went. Their appetite seemed quite insatiable; they could eat for days and nights on end, swelling out to two or three times their original size in a couple of days. One particular specimen which I had been watching for several days, a rare beauty striped like a tiger in bold yellow and black, had just reached what I thought was bursting point, and one day as I was breathlessly awaiting this moment, a bird suddenly whistled past my ear, dived through the web, and the spider was gone. He, too, must have been watching for some time, and may have thought that I had designs on his prey as well.

All that winter I patiently hunted for a snail's nest, but was never able to find one. As I still have not seen one to this day, I have to take it on trust that the mother snail (or rather the mother *half* of the creature, as snails enjoy the advantage of a two-way sex arrangement) digs a little hole in the ground where she lays her eggs, then seals it up carefully, and in the spring the nursery will swarm with minute pin-head babies crawling about blindly over one another (they only learn how to unfurl their eyes at a later stage of development). Unfortunately, my magnifying glass was not up to detecting one of these, although it did reveal one enthralling fact about a species which didn't scoop out a nursery, but carried its family on its head. You could see the tiny creature crawling about under a thin layer of skin on the mother's forehead. And I discovered that dragon-flies' mouths opened up sideways instead of up and down like ours, and that once their jaws were clamped together, the whole thing disappeared without trace, like a well-concealed trap-door.

The grasshopper, although furnished with a good brain and a splendid nervous system, is a slow learner, and you will have quite a job to teach him any tricks worth speaking of, unlike the cockroach and the circus flea, both of which are always anxious to add to their repertoire. When fully-grown the grasshopper kicks like a mule, as I once discovered when stroking one down the back to find out if he was ready to split out of his skin for his final moult. Having drawn blood, he then proceeded to puff himself up like a toad until the skin of his back ripped open like a burst paper bag. Fascinating creatures that they are, I was never able to resist their charm, and one day recently in Vence, as I was lovingly peering into my insect cage with a magnifying glass, our Jeannette, who comes in every day to smash a few plates, and considers it her business to keep the neighbourhood informed about our doings, couldn't resist asking me suddenly, 'Do you breed those beetles to feed to your cats?' And when I indignantly denied this, explaining that I merely wanted to *regarder* them, she gave me one of those pitying looks generally reserved for the mentally defective. A far cry from what Marie's reaction would have been!

10

AT SCHOOL, WE were tolerantly regarded as harmless freaks by our companions, whose judgement we accepted without question. And it says a great deal for them that we did not acquire a greater degree of inferiority complex than we did. In fact, enjoying school fort he first time, we¡ ived through that term in a kind of enchantment, floating a good six inches above the ground.

We had to be at school, four miles away from home, at eight o'clock in the morning. *Le petit tram*, which was a narrow-gauge open train, with curtains instead of built-up sides, picked us up every morning in St Georges at seven-thirty, and deposited us outside the school gates at ten minutes to eight. This just gave us time to dash through the hall out to the sandy schoolyard, and line up with our classmates. The teachers, who were known as *professeurs*, were all men. The boys were called by their surnames, but all the girls, down to the tiny eight year olds, were 'Mademoiselle'. Each *professeur* had his own room, so that we were constantly on the move from one classroom to another, according to the lesson which was coming up next. This made for an enormous amount of traffic on the stairs and in the corridors, endless crocodiles trudging in opposite directions, with a great deal of bantering and witty exchanges on the way. Little notes, love letters and *billets doux* changed hands constantly, assignations were made, and life was very exciting.

English boys become gallant at a much later age (if ever) than the French. Most of the boys in my class, although fierce and savage in their fights with one another, were gentle and attentive to us girls. They carried our books, gave us sweets, and let us copy their maths homework. And they chatted us up endlessly during break, with gracious compliments on the colour of our eyes and hair. The school yard, where all this went on, was an extension of the beach, shaded by umbrella pines, and the sound of the sea was always in the air.

At twelve o'clock we climbed back into the little tram, which was patiently waiting for us outside the college gates, and we puffed and whistled our way through the woods, back to the Villa Pépé for lunch. After which, stuffed and bloated with one of Marie's ample meals, we ambled back to our tram, and snoozed the rest of the afternoon away in the overheated college classrooms. Fortunately, the *professeurs* had also had a substantial lunch, and a great deal of their morning ardour had evaporated with the fumes of their daily bottle of claret or burgundy. Some of the wilder boys flicked ink pellets at the ceiling with impunity, or quietly unscrewed all the bolts of the bench in front of them, so that its occupant would suddenly crash to the floor with a frightful clatter. And sometimes a stink bomb would go off in the aisle, causing a fearful commotion, with everybody rushing to the windows for air. The four o'clock bell caused a stampede, with all decorum gone to the wind, and everybody leapt and pelted down the stairs, swinging satchels, and bellowing and whooping with released high spirits.

At that time, one of the clever girls in my class took me under her wing, and helped me tirelessly with homework and moral support. Day after day she enjoined me patiently not to get disheartened, and when I took her home to tea, she even talked

[68]

wisely to my mother on the subject. A year older than myself, she had a club foot, a cool brain and a very persevering nature. And remembering her with affection and gratitude, I have often wondered what became of her. She should by rights be teaching French literature in a senior girls' school somewhere in France. Her parents were abroad, and she and her sister shared a little house in the woods with a governess. It was a pleasant household, calm, cultured, cosy, sensible, and with all the right values. All three of them, I realised even then, were born spinsters.

Another girl in my form who could not be ignored, was a little hell-cat half my size, who had all the boys in the class under her control. I used to watch her giving them orders to persecute me, and wait and see what would happen. As I was totally unpractised in this kind of warfare, my only defence, prompted by instinct, was to emulate animals who feign death in the face of danger. When I saw it coming, I simply looked as pathetic and defenceless as I could—and this in fact was no act. All I had to do was to let my feelings show through. And it worked like magic. Even her most devoted slaves hesitated to attack such a poor, terrified-looking creature. As they approached, I dropped a handkerchief, or a ruler, and one of them would pick it up, and hand it back to me with a shamefaced grunt. Then they all slunk away to take their punishment. And although she kept this up for a whole term, I wasn't molested once. After the Christmas holidays, she either got bored with the game, or found another victim, and I was left in peace.

That autumn Danielle Darrieux, the film star, had launched the fashion for black *ciré* (an early form of plastic) raincoats, and we all wore them, boys and girls alike, whatever the weather. Those black raincoats, black gum boots and black berets were the uniform without which we would not allow ourselves to be seen, so that in a school where there was no regulation uniform, we put ourselves into one, of our own free will.

[69]

II

THAT WINTER WE started a weekly magazine, for which we soon received so many orders that we had to spend our entire time working on it. In those days there was a children's newspaper called *Benjamin*, to whose editor we sent a copy of our first number. He gave us a glowing write-up, which started the ball rolling, and the subscriptions came pouring in. The wretched thing, which was such fun to begin with, got out of hand completely, and soon became a menace. Had we been a little older and more experienced, we might have been able to run it efficiently, on a business-like basis. As it was, we wrote it all out by hand in block capitals with a special ink. The master copy was then pressed on to a kind of solidified jelly which absorbed the text, and from this jelly we could pull off as many sheets as we needed. We ran two serials, one short story, a crossword puzzle, nature 'notes' based on some of my observations of insect life, a fashion feature and a page of advertisements (fake to start with). The whole being copiously illustrated, it took a great deal of time to set it up, and thinking of the work involved, at fifty centimes a copy it was cheap at the price. We kept it up for six feverishly industrious months, at the end of which, exhausted and distracted, we had to give it up, writing to our subscribers that we were regretfully discontinuing publication for the time being, as school, alas, had to come first, and there was no time for both in our lives.

For several weeks after that I continued to wake up in the middle of the night in a cold sweat, thinking that I still had to dash off a couple of chapters for the serials before breakfast. Worst of all were the crossword puzzles, and for months we never dared move out of sight of a dictionary. But on the whole, in spite of the frenzy, I think we got more fun out of it than misery.

The next craze which came to pass was for bicycles. *Le petit tram* was suddenly considered cissy, and only fit for toddlers and grannies. So Mamma obligingly bought us a bicycle each, and from then on, we cycled to and from the college every day, come rain come shine. We either took the path through the wood, where a stream had to be crossed on a narrow wobbly plank, from which I once fell off, splashing, bicycle and all, into the water, on my way *to* school, so that I had to sit throughout the morning lessons steaming gently in my sodden clothes. Or else we went by the sea road which took longer, but was lovely on sunny days. On the way home from school, we often trundled our machines on to the beach at low tide, and raced round and round on the hard, wet sand, like swallows wheeling and circling low at sunset. In time, we devised a game of bicycle polo which we played with tennis balls and golf clubs. We dealt one another the most murderous blows, and crashed full-tilt into each other's front wheels. We often had to carry our bikes home on our backs, with the front wheels twisted into a figure of eight. That winter, all our pocket money went on repairs and 'new' second-hand wheels.

Another sport which we longed to practise, but could seldom afford, was sand-sailing. Little boats made of canvas and equipped with three bicycle wheels, a mast and two enormous sails, could be hired in Royan by the hour. In a high wind, these thistledown vehicles simply flew along the sands, and you needed a certain skill and a great deal of nerve to control them, and prevent them from taking off into the sky like a kite.

Christmas that year was ruined by chicken-pox. When the Darlanges arrived for the holidays, we all set off to the woods with saws and choppers to cut down the finest tree that we could find, and I had to swear on my honour, when Mamma eyed me suspiciously, that my swollen red ears, bloodshot eyes and whistling breath were symptoms of excitement pure and simple, and had nothing to do with the state of my health. We returned after several hours with a magnificent specimen, ten foot high and at least six across, which we packed into the huge zinc 'lessiveuse' in which the sheets were boiled every week, and we set up this splendid affair in the dining-room. By this time my face was closely peppered with spots, and no amount of swearing on my honour would do any good. To bed I had to go, and I can still remember with acute vividness the misery and despair at being banished from the party. Missing the feast had nothing to do with it. In fact when Marie brought me some turkey and plum pudding I was quite unable to eat it. But I cried into my pillow at the sound of their revels wafting up the stairs. Excitement and high spirits were their only stimulants, as wine or any form of alcoholic drink was still absolutely forbidden to us—not only on moral grounds, but because of their disastrous effect on growing bones and teeth which, my mother was convinced, would be softened to a jelly by their influence.

To cheer me up the next day, Jacques gave me a copy of Kipling's *The Light that Failed*, which he had received as a Christmas present, and which he thought would be much more useful to me, lying idle in bed all day long. And it was in fact the first full-length book that I ever read in English. I must admit that if it had not been for the pox and the enforced boredom, I would never have got through it, either then, or now, or at any other time. But it served the useful purpose of convincing me that I could read English, which I would never have believed otherwise.

That year flashed by in a twinkle. School work, from being utterly incomprehensible to begin with, was becoming a little easier, and at the end of the Easter term, my ancient Latin master informed me that I now knew enough to keep the headmaster happy, and that our daily lessons could be discontinued. The poor man, who had worked even harder than I, was worn to a shadow, and longed to shed his dim-witted pupil and get back to his heresies. Our daily lessons had even included Sunday morning after church, and for those who can take it, I recommend the method as the best way of getting the hang of the language, its peculiar syntax, back-to-front constructions and divine rhythm. But not everybody will think it worth paying the price!

And then the term was over, and the Easter holidays brought the Darlanges back from Paris, and we were all in heaven once more.

On the beach, half-buried in the sand was a black, square shooting box known as a *tonne*, which had broken away from its moorings in the marshes, floated out to sea, and subsequently been washed up by the tide. This was one of our favourite meeting spots at the time. Crawling through the narrow shooting slit (the door was on the opposite side, buried in the sand), we huddled inside feeling cosy, safe and quite unassailable. We talked for hours on end, mostly about what we had done and the books we had read; we formed plans for the future, set the world to rights, and when talk dried up, we made up stories, no one being allowed more than a five minute stretch at a time.

John produced, as a surprise, some pipes which he had made for us out of bamboo canes, after which he handed round the tobacco, a careful blend of Indian and China tea. We stuffed our pipes with this concoction and lit up. Within a few seconds we

[73]

were coughing and spluttering as a thick cloud of smoke filled the *tonne*, kippering our eyeballs and scorching our tongues. For the sake of face we would have had to go on indefinitely, had someone not suddenly remembered that it was Easter Saturday and we would have to go to confession that evening. We gasped at the thought—all that smoking! The priest would smell us out! Unable ever to take to confession in the accepted form, as it seemed quite impossible ever to trot out *all* your sins (which would take all day and be too shaming anyway) it was simply a tiresome ritual which for some reason kept the grown-ups happy, when you rattled off vague things like being mean, selfish, rude, calling your brother an imbecile, and having wicked thoughts while saying your prayers. But *real* specific sins, for which you could be punished, such as smoking tea in home-made pipes, were carefully kept back and never divulged.

And so, after struggling through the shooting slit again, we raced home, where we found Mamma safely anchored to her wireless, trying to capture the six o'clock news through the squeaks and crackles of the 'atmospherics', as Marie used to call them.

Creeping up to her bedroom, we each took a swig of her eau-de-cologne, good strong powerful stuff which went down like fire, and would obliterate all traces of tea-smoke on our breath. After which, carefree and happy, we skipped off to church to rattle off our sham confessions.

The pipe craze only lasted for a week, after which we gave up smoking, all but Nadia, who progressed to *Gauloises*, for which, from then on, she scrimped and saved, and on which she spent every sou that she could get hold of.

At other times, as a change from the *tonne*, we went to the *palombière*, which was a pigeon-hide perched on top of the tallest pine-tree that ever grew. The local farmers and vineyard workers used it for shooting wood pigeons, or *palombes* as they were called, and which is to me one of the most beautiful words

[74]

My mother, aged seventeen.

Mamma soon after I was born.
Her dog is defending the place—no room for smelly babies here.

First day in St. Georges,
wet and scruffy but very happy.

John and I riding one of the cannons
at Monte Carlo, with Marie peering from behind.

A picnic in the hills behind Vence.
Marie in one of her large hats as usual,
Mamma in the dashing cloche at the far end.

Nadia and I at Nostram,
swamped by a gaggle of small cousins.

The swing which
Rubio rigged up behind
the Esterel.

Last day of freedom before
going to boarding school
in Paris. The small cousin
is unconcerned at my fate.

Christine among
the daisies at Mas Mistral,
aged about three.

John leaving for his Jesuit
college, rigged out in his
plus-fours and peaked cap.

John and Jacques on the beach.
When they realised they had been made
into a picture postcard they were so furious that
they bought up the entire consignment of 500 cards.

Our daily ordeal on the beach—gym with M. Coulon.

The fifty-mile beach
with treacherous undertow,
where we were forbidden
to paddle our canoes.

The reef, submerged at
high tide, stretched for
miles, harbouring all
manner of marine life.

Goodbye to our favourite
beach. 3rd September 1939,
the first day of the war.

When the beach was too hot,
Nadia and I pitched tent
under the trees for the day.

Jacques and I on leave in
Paris at the end of the war,
shortly before his death.

Jacques trying to
throw Nadia off the roof
of their house in Paris.

The Mas Mistral, west view.
(*Pen and wash by the author*)

in the French language. The tree, which was as smooth and straight as a telegraph pole, could only be climbed by swarming up nails which stuck out at either side, and took you all the way up to the hide, in the topmost branches. These nails, mostly old and rusty, worked loose in the bark of the tree, and often came away in your hands, if they didn't snap clean off under your feet. This once happened to me as I was nearing the top, so that I was left suspended, clinging for dear life to a couple of rusty nails, with legs flaying wildly in search of some support, thirty feet above the ground. Jacques, who was just above me, vaulted on to the platform and hauled me up by the scruff of my neck.

The hide was made for two people at the most, but we were seldom less than six, and it is a wonder that the worm-eaten floor-boards did not crumble under our weight. This possibility did occasionally cross our minds, but being perched up there above everything else, with a view of the whole forest and miles of coastline, with nothing above our heads but the clear blue sky continually streaked with flights of wild geese and duck, was so exhilarating that it was well worth taking the risk, while extra excitement was added when a high wind blew and tossed us about like a ship on a high sea.

The following term we made friends with a girl in my class called Yolande, and she joined in our bicycle polo games with great gusto, which surprised us a good deal, as she had a mature and dignified look which utterly disguised her inner wildness. Completely hemmed in by her family life, she lived in a small château on the hill behind Royan, a lonely, tidy, repressed life in a wing of her own, with an aquarium full of goldfish and a governess who neglected her dreadfully, only appearing at meals when she gobbled her food in a way which even *we* found revolting, then disappeared to her room without ever offering to help with our homework.

One spring evening, after leaving Yolande to her own homework and the silent company of her goldfish, we were free-wheeling downhill on our bicycles, and as we had enjoyed a particularly lively game of polo the day before, my front wheel, which had a pronounced twist, scraped the mudguard with a hideous noise. The brakes had dropped off during a head-on collision, and the only way I could attempt to slow down as we approached the main street running at right angles at the bottom of the hill, was by pressing my foot down on the front tyre as hard as I could. This usually worked well enough, but in this case, under the strain, the wheel flew off and bounced away into the traffic. My bicycle pitched forward and crashed on its nose, and I was hurled against a passing car, from which, to my surprise, I bounced off, and hit the corner of the house across the street. Luck was on my side. I landed on my hip bone instead of my skull, but the bicycle was smashed and flattened under the wheels of the car, which drove on as if nothing had happened. There was no point in scraping up the remains of the bicycle, and we left them there for the dustmen to collect. Dazed and shaken as I was, I could not have managed to walk the four miles back to the Villa Pépé, and John kindly gave me a lift on his luggage rack. It was difficult to explain to Mamma the nature of the accident which had written off my bicycle, but had left me without a scratch. Willing to suffer almost any amount of pain rather than have to go to the doctor, I did my best not to limp under her nose. She told me to go and get myself another second-hand bicycle, and to try and look after it better in future.

12

WHEN THE SUMMER holidays finally came and, the Darlanges having arrived, we were riding high on clouds of bliss, Mamma suddenly threw a bomb into our midst. She was going back to Malaya, taking Christine with her, and the three of us would have to go to boarding schools in the autumn! This sounded like a life sentence and Marie assured us that it would be far worse then Devil's Island. We fully believed her.

Our joy at being all together again having been somewhat dashed by the gruesome news, we tramped off to the *tonne* to discuss the matter. But the Darlange children who had grown even larger in the last few months, only just managed to squeeze through the slit. It was touch and go, but they finally made it, and we all squashed up inside as tightly packed as sardines. We were growing up and the boys, whose voices were breaking, uttered the most comical squeaks, which reduced us to helpless fits of giggles. Ninette's hair had grown into beautiful glossy waves bouncing down her back, much to Nadia's disgust, as she herself was never able to produce anything more than a few fluffy tufts around her ears, in spite of all the bottles of castor oil which she poured over it. Her hair, far from being her crowning glory, was her despair, the kind of wispy fuzz which usually grows on babies.

From then on, each day became so precious, that I remember almost every separate minute, into which we packed as much fun and enjoyment as could be squeezed out of ordinary every-day living. We got up as early as we could, most days at sunrise in fact, and went down to the beach to swim, roll in the dunes and build enormous sand fortresses, real models of the Bastille, the Tower of London, Richard Coeur-de-Lion's Château-Gaillard, and various other historical *place fortes*, until it was time for breakfast, which we ate in the garden either at the Villa Pépé or at Nostram. On our way home, we bought piles of newly-baked rolls and croissants, hot and crackling from the oven, and these, split in half and spread with butter, eaten under the mulberry trees with mugs of café-au-lait, made a welcome and satisfying breakfast. Then back to the beach we went. That summer, we had a craze for the 'hanging corpse' game. Sprawling shoulder to shoulder in cartwheel fashion, we scraped away a nice pitch of damp sand, flat and smooth for drawing on. Then, each in turn drew a line or a squiggle or whatever, until you had a gibbet, with a rope and corpse hanging from it. Like 'old maid', the idea was to avoid at any cost being last, so that all sorts of curlicues and appendages were added, nails and screws to the gibbet, twists to the rope, eyelashes to the corpse, and a fierce argument arose when someone gave him ear-rings. Pirates and sailors sometimes wore *one* ear-ring, but whoever had ever heard of two? When bored with the hanging corpse, we played the word game. This consisted of writing the first and last letter, and as many dashes as were necessary to make up the word in-between. You could cheat as much as you liked by changing the word in your mind, as long as the letters already down corresponded. Then sooner or later someone jumped up and ran down to the sea, and the whole pack leapt up and followed with whoops and yells and piercing screams.

[78]

One fine day, John and Jacques disappeared and shut themselves up in the garage at Nostram. We were forbidden to approach, but of course our entire time was spent outside the door, wailing and begging to be let in. Inside they hammered and banged and sawed, and we could not imagine what they were up to. Then on the third day, they flung the doors wide open for us to admire the fruits of their labours. And there on the floor lay the most elegant little white canoe you had ever seen; with lathes of pine wood and yards of canvas, painted stiff to keep the water out, they had made it themselves, to John's specifications. (He was, later, to build his own ocean-going yacht, which he sailed for many years in the China seas.) In a state of high excitement we carried it down to the beach, where it rode the waves like a swan. But what was the use of only one canoe? We clamoured for more, and they obligingly went back to work, and the garage became a regular boat factory. Eventually we each had our own, which we paddled about in the bay from dawn till dusk. But the greatest excitement came with the high tides, when we raced out to where the rollers began to heave out of the sea. Once there, we swung our canoes around with a violent flip of the paddle (which often capsized the boats) but with luck, we sometimes managed to climb onto a roller at the crucial moment when it was gathering speed, and then we simply flew into shore on the huge wave—our own home-made version of surf-riding. Sometimes our canoes were smashed in particularly heavy seas, and we were churned up, wrapped in yards of canvas, in the raging breakers, often bruised by the flaying woodwork and gashed by exposed nails. But these small accidents were of no importance when compared with the thrill and excitement of the sport. Our great ambition was to take our boats further up the coast to the *Grande Côte*, where for hundreds of deserted miles the empty beaches faced the open Atlantic and the undertow sucked you far out to sea, before washing you up again several hours later, quite drowned, unless some lucky shark had managed to catch you on the way. But we were forbidden to paddle, let alone *swim* on that stretch of coast.

Beach picnics were another joy, as Marie, remembering her early training in Australia, produced the most fantastic spreads, for which she took a great deal more trouble than for ordinary meals at the villa.

Laden with baskets and followed by Rubio, until his exile, equally burdened with hampers and boxes of table silver, she would settle down at the foot of the dunes, where the tamarisks dispensed a thin feathery shade (all that there was, anyway), and under her orders Rubio spread out the cloths, the rugs and the food. There were always fresh rolls and several kinds of *saucisson*, cold roast pork and chicken in aspic, big fat juicy tomatoes, egg and salmon pies, and cucumber and potato salads. Then came plum tarts and meringues, and bottles of fresh lemon juice were dug into the sand to keep cool.

After these enormous feasts, we were forbidden to go into the water for an hour, a rule which we regarded as quite unnecessarily old-fashioned and stupid, until we were forced by circumstance to change our minds. Once, as we lay in the sand, bloated and comatose, there was a commotion on the beach, and two girls of about eighteen were brought out of the sea and laid on the sand. And although M. Coulon and the life-saving inspector sat on their chests and squeezed the water out of their lungs, the poor girls never came back to life. They were twins, who were staying with an aunt, while their parents were abroad. I shall never forget the poor aunt pacing back and forth between the two girls with her hands clasped, and praying aloud with tears streaming down her face. The girls, it appeared, had gone out in their canoes immediately after lunch, and capsized in a wave as we so often did ourselves, but instead of coming up for air, had sunk like stones to the bottom. After that, we stopped grumbling about the rule.

[80]

As summer progressed, we noticed a change coming over Jacques. He was growing moody, and, for no reason whatever, would suddenly snap at one of us girls, then go off for long walks by himself, if John was busy and refused to go with him. It was very tiresome, as it broke up the perfect harmony which had existed until then. The stupidest things would annoy him, and if he suddenly came across Nadia and me giggling helplessly over a croissant, which we were both nibbling from either end —or if we were reading the same book aloud, in different tones of voice, breaking off from time to time to hoot with laughter at our own wit, he would burst into the most awful rages and stamp away, banging doors. Finally, one day, he took me aside, and lectured me on the subject. It was time, he said, that we should begin to behave in a more grown-up way. It was all very well for Nadia to go on being a silly little girl (my dearest, most amusing, witty, intelligent friend, a silly little girl!!), but it was time for me to become more serious-minded, as I was, after all, a year older than she. This put me into a painful quandary, loving him devotedly as I did, and knowing that one day we would be married (this was assumed, as a matter of course, by everybody) I naturally wanted to keep him happy, but the thought of giving up all the fun that Nadia and I had together, was more than I could bear. This developed into a guilt feeling, and whenever she and I went off together in one of our dotty moods, I knew that I was in some way letting old cross-patch Jacques down.

Nadia always went to bed in great style. To ensure a maximum audience, she retired very soon after dinner and got into one of her sophisticated night-dresses, with shoulder straps and sides split up to the thighs. As we had never seen anything but our own long-sleeved high-necked vyella or tobralco night gear, these glamorous garments of hers dazzled and enchanted us. A great deal of time was spent in the bathroom with dogs perching and sprawling everywhere and Anne, Ninette and I sitting on the edge of the bath like a row of swallows on a telephone wire. Our role was to admire, advise and exclaim, as she puffed out those few hairs of hers, darkened her moles, sprayed herself with scent, and tried out interesting expressions in front of the glass. When we were satisfied that perfection had been reached and no further improvement was possible, she swept out of the room with one of those well-practised expressions on her face, and closely followed by the snuffling, snorting dogs we escorted her to her room. We never knew until the last minute which bedroom would be selected, or which one of her young cousins would be turned out and sent off to sleep in her own bed.

When a decision had been reached, she would get into bed, and pick up whichever book was in the running at the time, Victor Hugo or Racine, or Corneille (she was particularly scornful of these three) and she would read aloud in mocking tones as we sat on her feet, in fits of laughter. Sometimes, when she was feeling very magnanimous, we would be invited to squash in with her, squealing and giggling, with all the dogs scrabbling and scratching on top of us, barking their heads off, not knowing why, but feeling they had to. If she happened to have chosen a four-poster there was plenty of room, but when she occupied a short narrow child's bed it was a tight fit, and we screeched and squirmed and giggled in a lunatic frenzy. Sometimes, attracted by the noise, Jacques would walk in, shoulders and eyebrows raised in outraged disapproval. He glared at us, and stalked out growling, '*mais vous êtes folles, complètement folles,*' and I knew that I would be in for another lecture in the morning.

Sometimes he would tackle my mother, or she him, I never knew which way round it was, but I hated those long chats they had together, as it was perfectly obvious that they were discussing my shortcomings, and that Mamma was trying to enlist his help in improving me. Lectures invariably followed these dreaded tête-à-têtes, and although I knew he was quite right, it was intensely provoking to get the same kind of pie-jaw from him as from my mother. I suppose they thought it was high time for me to become a tidy, responsible and domesticated young woman. This had, alas, the opposite effect, and my efforts to improve slackened rather than increased. I knew I was untidy, lazy, selfish, terribly absent-minded (a great crime, this) and did not take enough trouble with my appearance—but whose fault, pray, was that, when I still wasn't allowed a looking-glass in my bedroom, and had to wash my face with scrubbing soap?

Then a cousin of Jacques, who lived in the Dordogne, came to stay at Nostram for a few days and joined in all our activities. Very tall, with dark, curly hair and soft, dreamy black eyes, he wore a brown woollen shepherd's cloak right down to the ground, which gave him the romantic look of a nineteenth-century poet. We all got on very well, so that after he left I was surprised to get a lecture from Jacques. 'You were flirting with him all the time,' he said accusingly. 'You shouldn't encourage him like that, you know. It's not fair.' I was stunned. *Had* I encouraged him? I tried to remember. Once we had sat in the dunes together, chatting about school. Another time, on our way back from a long walk, when a cold wind had sprung up, he had taken me under his shepherd's cloak, with his arm around my shoulder. To be honest, I had to admit that perhaps I *had* encouraged him. I could have insisted on freezing all the way home, instead of snuggling cosily inside his cloak. I suppose I looked contrite because Jacques said kindly, 'Don't worry, never mind. He won't come back again.' And he was right. He never did.

On rainy days, we all huddled upstairs in one of the bed-rooms, and the choice was always according to the mood of the moment. The gun dogs followed us from room to room, patiently padding after us, then jumped up onto whichever bed we settled, their great wide paws splayed on our bare legs, leaving white claw scratches on the sunburn. Their fleas hopped about in voluptuous abandon, and nobody paid them any attention. Nadia would get hold of some ludicrous novel, and read aloud the purple passages and love scenes while we, shaking with suppressed laughter, performed the actions in a kind of silent charade. The silence never lasted very long, as someone exploded sooner or later, at which everybody joined in. But woe betide us if Jacques suddenly appeared in the midst of one of these childish games. After the usual outburst of rage at our silliness, he would plod off moodily into the rain, and return covered with mud, and in a worse temper than ever. The only way to soothe him was to get our paints and stories out, and settle down at the dining-room table and start scribbling away. In a few minutes he would come and sit beside me, and pick up a paint brush himself. I would read out the last chapter I had written, and he produced one illustration after another with amazing rapidity. His figures and animals were so alive that they practically jumped off the paper.

When a chapter was finished, we reversed the roles, he wrote the next instalment, while I struggled with the drawings. We were writing a long rambling story about a cave man, his hunts, his fights with other cave men, and finally the capture of a beautiful cave girl clad in a bearskin. It was all as corny as could be, and enormous fun to do, filling two exercise books, and invaluable as a pacifier of Jacques' ferocious moods. Sometimes we worked at Nostram, but the constant interruptions irritated him beyond endurance, particularly as he knew how much I enjoyed them. One small cousin after another would burst in with a request for a piece of string to mend a shrimping net, or sticking plaster for a lacerated knee, or simply an offer to help with our painting. And best of all, Nadia made an occasional pounce, and dragged me away to impart some secret of the most urgent nature. So, on the whole, Jacques much preferred to work in our villa. We spread our materials on the table in the garden, and soon Marie would come out with glasses of lemon juice or cups of tea, into which he frequently dipped his brush, just as he often took a swig of the paint water, without ever noticing the difference.

When we ran out of inspiration, he would take a book out of his pocket and read aloud. When the Mowgli books, which we both loved, had been read several times over, he found *Nils Holgersson* by Selma Lagerlof, and this enchanting Nordic tale kept us under a spell for several weeks.

The summer slowly, imperceptibly drifted into autumn, 'our last summer', as we called it, and as the sun grew less hot on the beach we began to roam the countryside, picking great baskets of blackberries, which we brought home for Marie to make into jams, jellies, moulds and fools. Elderberries ripened much at the same time, and these we also picked to be turned into a delicious thick black goo which never quite jelled, but produced the most haunting and subtle smell while it was cooking.

Gradually, as the time approached for my imprisonment, I grew at last more serious-minded, and began to detach myself from the others, and to accompany Jacques on his lonely walks. His temper improved noticeably, and he became much kinder and more patient. This was a great relief.

13

ON OCTOBER 1st, 1935, my mother, my school trunk and I climbed into a taxi, and screeched and hooted our way through the streets of Paris on our way to Vincennes, where my new school was awaiting my arrival.

For the first time in our lives we were split up. Anne was packed off to a dark and gloomy dungeon in a small provincial town in the Gironde, from which it was amazing that she survived, John went off to Sarlat, a Jesuit college, where he had to wear plus-fours and a peaked cap like a chauffeur, and I was put down for Sévigné, which promised to turn me from the wild country creature that I was, into what a *demoiselle de bonne famille* ought to be. And judging from the others' tales, I was by far the luckiest of the three.

Sévigné, which was by a strange coincidence the name of the first school we ever attended in Vence, was surrounded by walls fifteen feet high, so that the elegant eighteenth-century building behind them was quite invisible from the street. It was a small château which, as I discovered later, had belonged to one of the famous royal mistresses (whose identity I forget), and the enormous cedar tree in the *cour d'honneur* was where la Fontaine used to come and read his fables to her before they appeared in print. The château had been built over the ruins of a very much older building, so that the basement, in which much of our life was spent, was a low-ceilinged, stone-floored crypt supported by arches and pillars. It was firmly believed by all of us that the floor was made of tombstones, under which lay the remains of centuries of monks. We knew perfectly well that at midnight their ghosts oozed out of the floor and drifted about, groaning and wailing and rattling their beads.

We were ushered on arrival into the salon of the headmistress, in the centre of which she was standing, drawn to her full height of at least five feet. Though a head shorter than me, she was *une très grande dame*. In the dress of an abbess, she must have looked formidable, and even in her long everyday black gown with leg-of-mutton sleeves and high lace collar, she managed to be imposing. Since the separation of Church and State, nuns were forbidden to teach, so they got round it by wearing mufti. Everybody knew of the deception, but as long as appearances were kept up, and the nuns wore what they thought was 'ordinary' modern dress, the Ministry of Education allowed them to carry on unmolested. There were only three lay teachers in the school, but even they were in secret training for convent life.

As I shook hands with the headmistress, I felt my wrist being wrenched downwards in a grip of iron, so that I found myself almost down on one knee. My mother, who had never seen me do such a thing before, stared in amazement, but she could not have been more surprised than I. It was my first introduction to the perpetual round of curtseys which went on all day long throughout the school. The 'worker-nuns' curtseyed to us as they handed the dishes round at meals, or when we met them in the corridors; we curtseyed to the teachers, and everybody curtseyed to the headmistress, and also of course to M. Le Chanoine, who now slowly emerged from the shadows like the

Cheshire Cat. He would, I was told, have to hear my sins in future. Weekly confession was compulsory, one of the iron rules of the school.

Another rule was that pupils were only allowed to receive letters from parents, and all correspondence, incoming and out-going, was read and censored by the headmistress herself. Unsuitable letters would be burned. If anyone was caught trying to smuggle a letter out of the school, immediate expulsion would follow. The list of rules was read out, while the grown-ups sat stonily on their chairs—no seat was provided for me. I stood in the middle of the floor.

After this we were dismissed, and a worker-nun conducted Mamma and myself to the hall, where we said goodbye. The worker-nun then took me along endless corridors to my cubicle in the dormitory, where she left me, kindly saying that I could cry until the dinner bell, but that afterwards no more signs of emotion would be allowed.

The dormitory, which was like a warehouse—small, square windows high up near the ceiling let in the only light—contained eighty beds, each surrounded by white curtains. At the four corners were larger cubicles for the *surveillantes*. No talking was allowed of course, either in the dormitory or the wash-rooms, where we each had an enamel bowl and a can of water. These were placed on a shelf running all the way round the room, so that we decently faced the wall as we washed. This had to be somehow achieved under the dressing-gown, so that not an inch of bare flesh could be seen. A *surveillante* stood in the centre of the room to make sure that no indecency (such as a dressing-gown accidentally slipping to the floor) should occur.

Friday was foot-bath night, a welcome break in the routine of the week. This took place in the basement, in an enormous low-ceilinged crypt held up by a multitude of pillars. Between these were benches and tin basins. We sat on the benches and paddled our feet in the basins, while little worker-nuns scuttled around with cans of hot water. In complete silence, we soaked and scrubbed, modestly keeping our skirts down. Then we dried our feet, which felt warm and spongy, struggled back into our black stockings, and filed into the refectory for our special Friday evening dinner of turnips and boiled cod.

Altogether, the morning and evening wash, and Friday foot-baths, were the only scrubbing which most of the girls got throughout the term. I, along with five others, all rather spoilt, were allowed a weekly bath. This was an extra, and considered dangerous to the health so that the school doctor (a very old man with a little grey beard growing out of each of his ears) had to be consulted every time. 'And why, mademoiselle,' he asked me once, 'do you have to have such a mania for baths? It is not normal to be obsessed to this point!' But he only refused permission once, when I had a sore throat and wheezing tubes.

The refectory was an enormous room in the crypt, next to the foot-bath. There were naturally no windows. A long table shaped like a horseshoe ran all round the room between two rows of pillars. Plates only were laid, as our own table silver, including mugs, was wrapped in our napkin and tucked away on a little shelf underneath the table. When the meal was over, tin basins filled with boiling water were placed at intervals along the table, and we all plunged our mugs and cutlery into it, using our napkins as drying-up cloths. Only the dirty plates were left to be rushed away by the worker-nuns. And although I fail to see how this was training me from my previous state of half-savagery to the manners of a *demoiselle*, it was certainly a neat way of dealing with the washing-up problem.

Everybody fussed about the food, but I always found it delicious. All the meals, except breakfast of course, started with soup, then came the meat handed round by the nuns, and eaten with bread. This was followed by a vegetable, always cooked as a special course on its own, and finally cheese and fruit were put on the table. Bananas had to be eaten with a tea-spoon, and apples, pears and peaches with a knife and fork. And *what* a business that was! The senior school (from the age of twelve upwards) had a carafe of wine and water between six people, as part of the menu, but butter was an extra.

After grace we went back to the prep room for an hour, then off to the chapel to say the entire rosary on our knees, and finally to bed. At six thirty the next morning we were back in the chapel for mass, during which everybody was expected to take communion (you stood out like a sore thumb if you didn't), after which came breakfast, consisting of bread and cocoa. My mother, in the kindness of her heart, had said that I could have butter as well.

By eight o'clock we were in our classrooms, with more praying to ask for the blessing of Heaven on the morning's work. Most of the time we simply gabbled through the 'work prayers' as quickly as possible, hoping for the chance of a quick squint at our books before we had to say our lessons.

Our form mistress, who was one of the non-nuns, but none the less holy for that, always started with 'Mesdemoiselles, I am ready to serve you. Please sit down.' Like all the other teachers, she upheld the fiction that the staff were our paid servants, and were there to do our bidding at all times. This was infuriating, as they knew as well as we did that nobody was fooled. The headmistress our servant my foot! Why and when this idiotic theory started I have no idea, and possibly it was true at some point in the history of the school, but by the time I was there, it was certainly a big fraud.

Two male teachers actually penetrated the establishment and taught the senior school. One was the literature master, and the other taught Greek and Latin. They came into the classroom flanked on either side by a couple of lay-nuns, who both sat beside him throughout the lesson. We often wondered what these old men might have got up to if left alone with us, but it was beyond the imagination of even the most knowing of my classmates.

After lunch and tea, we were allowed out in the garden for half an hour when the weather was fine. Otherwise we stayed indoors in the prep room, which, like schools all over the world, smelt of dust, ink and pencil shavings.

The last half-hour before supper was spent in the company of our form mistress, who was known as Holy Jo (Jojo-la-Pieuse, actually, as her name was Johana) and who was preparing herself to take the veil. She probably had a true vocation, but we, with our pedestrian outlook, were convinced that she had been disappointed in love. She read improving books to us aloud while we day-dreamed drowsily at our desks, and then tried to sort out our troubles and grievances by an insidious form of questioning (not to say prying) which we resented very much. Also we didn't altogether trust her. So much resignation, renunciation and holy 'offering up' cloyed around the gills, so that you longed to throw open the windows and let the cold clean sharp air knife its way through all that mushy nia-nia stuff to the hard, bare bone.

In the garden we played croquet or quoits, in what had been at one time gravel, but was now dust or mud, according to the time of year. We were forbidden to gather in groups of less than four, and when only two were caught conferring together, they were sent indoors to learn a fable. Consequently it was very difficult to make friends. I tried to chum up with my next-door neighbour in the dormitory, but the only idea she had in her head was to get married in order to beget as many sons as possible, for the sole purpose of killing Germans. This, she was convinced, was her patriotic duty, and she was determined to accomplish it. Circumstances thwarted her, however, as the war came far too soon for her plan to be carried out.

If there were any kindred spirits, it was impossible to seek them out, as the opportunities for coming together were practically non-existent. At meals, we managed to communicate to some extent by using the sign language of the deaf and dumb, but as all those in authority, down to the humblest worker-nun, knew it as well as we did, we were never free to 'say' what we wanted. Sometimes, as I looked around at the sullen, silent faces of my companions, I could not help thinking that surely, somewhere, there must be *some* happiness left. And of course there was. One whole day of it, which stands out in my memory like a luminous impressionist painting. May Day, although the official communist jamboree, was also, for some inexplicable reason, kept as a holiday by our very reactionary school. We were bundled into coaches in which we were actually allowed to *talk*, and driven to St Germain-des-Prés, where every inch of ground was so thickly covered with lilies of the valley as to look like snowfields. The bright hot sun and the scent of the flowers went to our heads and we went quite mad, running around and chasing one another like hysterical hens. The calls to order and the whistles of the staff had no effect whatever, and it was only when quite exhausted that we calmed down, and began to pick the flowers. Each one of us brought back a huge bunch, all of which of course had to go to the chapel.

Our uniform was the same winter and summer so that, as it was adequate in winter, we simply sweltered in July, which can be *very* hot in Paris. It consisted of a sailor suit of heavy blue serge, with a pleated skirt and black stockings. For Sunday we had the same, but in white. Navy blue felt hats completed the ensemble.

Our gym gear had to be seen to be believed—navy blue knickerbockers to just below the knee with over them a wide flounced skirt like a lampshade, banded with white, a sailor suit blouse also banded with white, and for the head a triangular piece of cloth tied up in front like a turban, into which all the hair had to be tucked. Decked out in these incredible togs, we marched round and round the foot-bath room, from which the benches had been removed. The gym-nun, whose teeth kept falling out so that she constantly had to catch them in her handkerchief, clapped her hands together as we marched. And that was our gym lesson.

Gloom and depression settled on me that term, and bored their way into my spirits, which had never been so low before. It was, when I think of it now, the dreary lack of anything exciting, or even interesting, ever happening, the stifling, joyless atmosphere, and the feeling that one was always suspected of doing something wrong. Just once, a girl who had grown desperate, made a dash for it by trying to bolt past the 'porter-nun', while something was being delivered. She was hauled back by the hem of her skirt, and we never saw her again. There was a rumour that she had been pushed down an *oubliette* in one of the dungeons, but this was only wishful thinking, as we knew perfectly well that nothing so exciting could ever happen in our dump.

Christmas that year was a dismal failure. My mother and Christine had left for Malaya after dumping us in our various schools, and apart from the joy of seeing Marie and John and Anne again (all of them were even more miserable than I), the Villa Pépé was cold and gloomy beyond belief. Poor Marie, who missed Christine dreadfully, did her best to rouse our spirits, but she was too low herself to do any of us much good. The Darlanges stayed in Paris, so that we were alone in St Georges. We went for listless walks, and quarrelled incessantly. We would really have been much happier in Vence, and I can't think why it didn't occur to Marie to take us there. The only bright spot during the holidays was Kipling's *Captains Courageous* which I received as a Christmas present, and which transported me far, far away into a completely different world. I read it three times before going back to school.

The misery of that year stands out like a black tunnel, and

when a telegram arrived from Malaya, telling us all to go to England by the next boat, it came as a great relief. As I found out later, the Hilliers, our ex-neighbours from Vence, were behind this move. It was high time, they wrote to my mother in Malaya, that we should go to English schools, as no education existed outside England. My mother, who had no trouble at all in swallowing that, acted at once, and I can imagine her writing out the telegram and despatching the estate postman off on his bicycle with it.

14

JOHN WAS SENT to Douai, from which he escaped within half an hour of his arrival, and Anne and I were bundled off to Rosemead, in Littlehampton.

It was a revelation. The relaxed relationship between the staff and the girls never ceased to amaze me. When my desk neighbour once said to the geography mistress, 'Oh Miss Throup, you *are* a pig!' I nearly fell off my chair. Particularly as the only retaliation elicited by the remark was a good-natured clip over the ear with a notebook.

And then we were *trusted*. It was assumed, on all occasions, that we would tell the truth. At Sévigné we had been spied upon through every hour of the day, and the feeling that someone was always trying to catch us out never let up. The enmity between the staff and the girls was continually sustained and nourished by small meannesses on both sides.

At Rosemead, another amazing factor was the spirit of co-operation which pervaded throughout the school. The mistresses were tolerantly regarded as brainboxes with a tiresome job to do, and the girls ran the school. It was the prefects and the 'subs' job to organise games, outings, walks, runs, rehearsals, who assembled the school for prayers and who devised and enforced punishment for breaking the rules. 'Walking round the cabbage patch' for half an hour at a time was one of their favourites, as it was healthy exercise, kept you out of doors, and the victim could be watched from the dining-room windows.

Unbelievably were the school gates not only wide open at all times, but you were allowed out of the grounds, and into the town three at a time! To me, this was like looking at the world upside down, and a very agreeable aspect it had from that angle. I kept these continual shocks to myself, as I wanted above all else to be 'one of them', and to *appear* at least to take everything as much for granted as they did. From the start, Anne succeeded far better than I. She was good at games and quite fearless on the lacrosse field, whereas I, to my shame, turned out to be quite hopeless. The sight of a beefy-thighed Viking of a sixth-former bearing down on me across the field, brandishing her stick if ever I managed to get hold of the ball, terrified me beyond words, so that I flung ball and stick away blindly and fled. This went down very badly, and after several serious talks from the Head of the House, I was dropped out of the game and tacked on to the 'invalids' walk', which was made up of weak hearts, crashing bores and a pair of feeble-minded twins.

These dreary walks along the sea front in the biting East wind were very little pleasure. We had to keep in line, and were not allowed to run. There was no alternative to freezing almost to death. As my gloves were nearly always lost, and we were forbidden to put our hands in our pockets, the misery was un-mitigated, but we kept ourselves going with the thought of tea. Not a very grand one, but eagerly looked forward to, and very welcome when it came—bread and butter and cake one day and bread and butter and jam the next. Supper, on the other hand, was unbelievably insubstantial, and consisted of a plate of corn-flakes and an orange, which we had to collect ourselves (shades of the worker nuns scurrying around the refectory, waiting on us and bobbing and curtseying as they handed round the dishes!).

There were two headmistresses, 'Toby', who taught divinity so that, as an R.C., I was never in her class, and 'Nita', who did English literature with the sixth form. As a great treat, I was allowed to join this lesson while still in the fifth, and for the first time, owing to Nita, I realised that Milton was not the pompous and cumbersome bore I had always thought him to be. Most lessons were in fact enjoyable, and the teachers were easy-going, had a sense of humour and a refreshingly detached attitude towards us. I particularly liked the history mistress, who looked like a cod's head, with her shoulders running straight into her neck, and who didn't give a damn. She was fascinating to watch and listen to.

That year, I really took to Latin and Greek, which so impressed the heads, that a special classics master came over from Lewes to teach me. We both sat (*alone* and *without a chaperon*! I was stunned by this) in Toby's drawing-room, where we romped through Sophocles and Virgil with great gusto. He seemed to enjoy the lessons as much as I did. My colleagues thought me a nutcase, but as they had suspected it from the start, it did not make very much difference. The French mistress would not have me in her class, as she said it was unfair to the others (the fact that I lost a lot of marks by not being allowed to do any French at all did not seem in the least bit unfair to *her*), and I was a total failure in the arithmetic lessons, where I had no idea what it was all about. The teacher soon gave me up as hopeless, and allowed me to do my homework in her class. To this day I cannot understand why nobody thought of giving me extra coaching in this subject. Bred (in fits and starts) on the decimal system, English arithmetic was a deep and awesome mystery to me, and still is. Only since decimals were forced upon a reluctant Britain have I been able to cope with even the simplest household accounts.

[97]

'Prep', after tea, was two hours of enforced boredom. I had nothing to do as my homework was always done during the French and arithmetic lessons. I tried to write stories, but in that atmosphere of concentrated boredom—you could almost see it hovering over the bent heads of the school like a heat-haze—and without Jacques at my elbow to encourage and prod me along, writing bits in himself when the story got stuck, inspiration would not come. At that time, I missed him more than ever, and tried to imagine what he would make of the place if he ever turned up to visit me. But alas, he never did. The thought of Nadia as an inmate of the school was even more incongruous. With such thoughts and imaginings I did my best to while away the time. But it was definitely the worst part of the day.

As R.C.'s we had prayers separately in Nita's study, and these were conducted by the assistant matron, who swung a stiff arm. Everybody said it was made of wood from the shoulder down, but we never knew for certain. Among the Catholics was a girl called Anne Sainsbury, half-French like us, who had the great good fortune of being able to put her back out by bending over and touching her toes. Whenever she wanted to slide out of anything tiresome like church, or a spell around the cabbage patch, she would surreptitiously slip away, touch her toes and come back crowing 'All's well, it's out again, girls!' She would then retire to the sanatorium for a couple of days with a bundle of books from the library, and a pocketful of tuck. We very much envied her this useful talent. During the war she distinguished herself by doing heroic work in the French Resistance, and once, when shot in that back of hers, stoically submitted to the extraction of the bullet without anaesthetic.

In our Rosemead days she was in Anne's form, and they were both great friends.

After church on Sunday came the dreaded letter-writing period, which kept us imprisoned in our classrooms until lunch. Looking around, and running through the cosy monotony of our days in my mind, comparing it with their exciting and colourful life in Malaya, I could not think of anything to say that might possibly interest my parents, and so I spent the letter-writing hour gazing at the window and chewing the wooden holder of my relief nib. When it was time, in due course, for my own daughter to go to boarding school (at her request—'You might as well face it, mummy, *everybody* goes to boarding school in England!') *she* was never short of news, and wrote letters which went like this.

> 'To my darling mother,
>   Corner Two,
>   Slough of Despond,
>   Worry World.
> It is absolutely terrible here. The girls are horrible; they gang up and giggle behind my back because they think I am innercent. It's not fair if they only knew I have a mind like a dusspin.
> My coat is covered with sticky spots as the silly mare I milked in the New Forest this afternoon for the rabbits supper jerked her udder at the wrong moment and splashed milk all over my face and coat.
> Please send a knife small enough to put under my pillow to kill Jenny in the middle of the night. I hate her with my whole guts.
>
>   Your only beloving daughter.'

Unfortunately, as I had neither her imagination nor her fluency, I could think of a great many other things I would much prefer to do, such as digging in my garden. The summer term was utterly delightful. We were roused at seven o'clock, but allowed to get up as early as we liked and I was usually prowling around the grounds by five-thirty. It was the best time of the day, when the white sky looked as if no cloud could ever soil it, and the birds, pecking around for their breakfast, chattered confidentially to one another, comparing notes on what the morning had to offer, with an occasional squeak of excitement when something particularly juicy turned up. I always hoped they would stay away from the willow trees, in and out of which we played that popular game of Cocky Oliver, and which was the haunt of the gallant and colourful puss-moth with its bright red cheeks, and its curious habit of standing on end and waggling its tail feathers at you if he considered you were taking liberties I think even the birds thought twice about *that* particular morsel.

As I was useless at lacrosse they assumed I would be equally hopeless at tennis, and the games prefect invariably paired me off with the feeblest-minded twin, so that I never had a chance to learn. Soon the twin had to be dropped out altogether, and I was told I could have the time to myself. This was pure bliss, as I could spend the afternoons lying in the long grass in a cosy coma, listening to the busy life of the soil and all the sounds of summer, the girls' voices on the courts shouting fifteen-love, thirty-all, deuce, game, oh you pig, and all the usual endearments which school girls reserve for one another. From time to time I learnt a stanza of Kubla Khan, or the Lady of Shallott, or one of the Odes of Keats, as a sop to my conscience, which niggled me a little about being so very idle. English poetry I found perfectly lovely, far, far more entrancing than any of Lamartine's most romantic effusions, and even the *farouche* Vigny lost some of his shine, when compared with the roll and rollick of Browning.

'Heaven lies about us in our infancy, The prison walls begin to close around the growing boy', said Wordsworth, who obviously knew. Was this, I wondered, what had happened to Papa? Immured in his inner fortress, completely shut off from the outside world, quite desperate and alone, he could not, or so it seemed, and try as he might, make contact with another soul. And his voice, coming from so far away, where his being lay buried behind the prison walls, was thin and weak and infinitely sad. How very terrible it must be for some people to grow up. The pity of it quite twisted my heart. Would it also happen, I wondered, to the growing girl? I hoped very much that it would not. But I was far from sure.

The brightest twin cornered me one day, and asked me to become her sister's keeper. I suppose that she wanted a break from the job herself, and, not wanting to slap her down on the spot, said that I would think about it. From that moment on, the feeblest twin attached herself to me with doglike persistence, shambled up every morning before breakfast to present her hair, teeth and nails for inspection, then followed me docilely down to the dining-room. During the dreary sea-front walks she gripped my hand, as she was inclined to topple over, and I always openly did her homework for her. As an arrangement, the teachers and the prefects seemed to find it perfectly satisfactory. Relief from this unremitting servitude came only after a year, when the twin got pneumonia and was sent to Switzerland to recover.

On the first day of June, come rain come shine, the entire school went down to the beach to bathe. The thought of a swim in the sea again made my knees wobble with excitement, but very soon they were rattling together for a very different reason. The East wind, roaring across land and sea all the way from Manchuria, turned our flesh blue as we undressed, our teeth chattered as the whistle blew us into the water, and we nearly died as we came out. But after a couple of weeks we toughened up, and although it never came up to the standard of St Georges, the agony lessened, and we learned to take it in our stride, along with the luke-warm baths in winter, the thin suppers, and the hungry nights.

Some of Rosemead's habits remained strange to me until the end. For instance, the girls always drew their cubicle curtains to say their prayers, which to me, used to kneeling in the dust in public as I was, seemed curious to say the least, particularly as they happily stripped to the skin, exposing themselves quite bare to one another without the slightest qualm. I soon learnt to say my own prayers behind drawn curtains too, but never, *never* was I able to undress in front of them.

Another thing which has remained incomprehensible to me to this day was the effect of the King's abdication, which swept over the school like a catastrophe of the greatest magnitude. They sobbed on their beds all the afternoon, and the head girl, that vast mountain of flesh who so terrified the lacrosse field, wept loudest of all, and cancelled all games for that day. Such was their grief that some of them could not even eat their evening cornflakes and I, the stony-hearted frog, dry-eyed and puzzled beyond words, gobbled up several extra suppers. It seemed to me no tragedy that the gentle-faced new King should take over a job which his brother so obviously detested. Had there been murder or foul play, as, for instance, in *Macbeth*, that of course would have been a different matter.

Half-way through our career at Rosemead my mother suddenly decided to bring Christine back from Malaya and submit her to the civilising influence of Europe. Bright, active, quick-witted, and as ignorant as the usual run of Fesq children, far more enterprising than we had ever been at her age, and unrestrained by Marie's ever-watchful fierceness, she lived, in Malaya, a life of great freedom, and made full use of her opportunities. Nimble as a wild-cat, she could run up a coconut tree as well as any of the native children, whom she had dragooned into a well-disciplined army which she marched around the plantation, training them in jungle warfare and survival exercises. Herons and other birds, killed in full flight with well-aimed stones, were roasted on camp fires which spread underground along the infinite network of dead roots and rotted vegetation, causing the most appalling risk of forest fires. So, what with one thing and another, the time had come for poor

Christine to be tamed and deprived of her wild-animal freedom.

They arrived after Christmas, at the coldest, bleakest time of the year, and my mother rented a terrible little house, with hardly any garden, in St Flora's Road, two minutes away from Rosemead. The idea was that we should be able to go home every evening and stop being boarders. This was meant as a great treat, but in fact, by then, we thoroughly enjoyed the life of the school and hated the thought of being day-girls. There was, moreover, the usual snobbery branding day-girls as inferior beings. Since we felt that we were only just becoming integrated, being more or less accepted as harmless oddities from another world, it seemed hard to have to be demoted again so soon. Neither Anne nor I ever discussed this, but each knew perfectly well what the other felt, and of course it was unthinkable even to mention it to my mother or anybody else, so day-girls we became, moving into the dreary little house, with its Times furnishing, antimacassars, art-nouveau lampshades, and countless other horrors. The first time that we were taken over to see it, a large, coal-black mammy, the departing tenants' cook, fled outside and tried in vain to hide behind the one and only spindly apple tree which the garden possessed, and in spite of our sinking hearts, we could not help laughing at the incongruous sight.

One redeeming feature was a piano, so that Mamma's singing sessions could be resumed. She tried hard to teach us, and we even had lessons at school, and how she, who had such a sensitive ear, could bear the dreadful noise we made, I cannot imagine. It must have been torture for her, but even though she showed no sign of it, we all had to recognise eventually that neither Anne nor I was *douée pour la musique*, and our efforts came to an end.

That winter I caught a cold which dragged on for weeks, and by ten o'clock at night, exhausted by the coughing, I crept up to bed, depressed and drained of all energy.

One evening after dinner, as I was crouching over my home-work, coughing and sniffling in Marie's sitting-room with its comforting rows of pickled snakes and frogs on the bookshelves (the only cosy room in the house), she suddenly said out of the blue, 'I'm sure you're consumptive. It's not normal to go on and on like this.' I stared at her in alarm. 'But,' I stammered, 'isn't that a deadly disease?' (Tuberculosis, or consumption as it was then called, was an almost certain killer in those days.)

'It certainly is,' she replied emphatically, 'I've met hundreds of them in Switzerland, lovely girls from all over the world, coughing their lungs up and hoping for a cure, all dead within a year. Nothing you can do about it.'

My insides turned over: 'Do you mean to say that I shall be dead within a year?' I asked.

'Most likely. Mind you, it's a painless death. They even say the worse you get, the happier you feel.' This was no consola-tion at all. My spirits dropped to zero.

'Never mind,' she said, as she saw me drooping, 'We all have to die sooner or later. And I will lay you out myself, and let nobody else touch you. My mother taught me how to do it, and she learnt it from *her* mother. Nowadays, people don't bother any more. They get strangers to lay out their dead. Disgusting, that's what I call it!' And unconscious of her ghoulish pun, she added, 'It's a dying art and no mistake,' then, looking at me thoughtfully, 'You will make a nice, neat little corpse. Just leave it to me.' My mind was reeling.

'How do you do it?' I asked. 'Tell me about it.' And she proceeded to do so, and so gruesome was the process that even now I cannot bring myself to write it down.

That night I cried myself to sleep at the thought of having to die so soon, and spent the next few days in terror of eternal damnation, as all the dreadful sins of my life kept popping into my head from the dark corners where they had lain decently hidden for so long.

Gradually the cough cleared up and my usual health and appetite returned, thereby robbing poor Marie of her treat. In fact she never had the chance of laying any one of us out.

15

THE GATEHOUSE WAS a bungalow in the grounds, where they kept the juniors up to the age of twelve, after which they were moved up to join us in the main part of the school. And so it was there that Christine was assigned when she arrived, and where she proceeded to practise her psychic powers, which she had presumably developed during her early jungle life and her dealings with the children of the estate coolies, and which appeared to work equally well with the inmates of the Gatehouse. At meals, having selected her victim, she would stare at her and think hard, 'put your hands on your head', and up would go the poor child's hands. Inanimate objects were equally amenable to her influence, and when she stared at the telephone saying fiercely, 'drop telephone, drop!' it would obediently hop off the table and crash to the floor.

And although she has now given up these childish pranks, she still keeps in constant touch with the spirit world, and gets endless messages and useful hints from the Other Side through a complicated system of smells. Tobacco means one thing and heliotrope another, and so on right down a long list which included about twenty smells when she sent it to me a few years ago, but there may have been additions since then.

During her Gatehouse days we saw very little of Christine, as she came home in time for tea, and was completely reclaimed by Marie, who was ecstatic with happiness at having her back, and they resumed their close, exclusive life together, very much apart from the rest of the family.

John, who had managed his affairs remarkably well, had found his way to a very easy-going, happy-go-lucky cramming establishment run by a foreign baron in Arundel. This suited us all very well, as he could come home whenever he liked, any time during the week, as well as every weekend. And when the Easter holidays started and my mother bought us a fisherman's boat with a mast and sails, which we kept in Littlehampton harbour, life began to show signs of regaining some of its early shine and splendour.

As we had never done any sailing before, we all thought it wise to have a little practice in the harbour, before sailing out to the big wide open sea. So for a few days, we tacked up and down the estuary, getting in everybody's way and frequently ramming the sandbank on the golf course side of the river. After a few days of these aquatic cavortings, we felt as confident as a bunch of old salts, and decided to set out to sea. But so ignorant were we of the local conditions that we had no knowledge of the Bore, which made it impossible to get out of the river by sail alone, and without an outboard motor. We had thought that we would float out with the current like a piece of driftwood. A fishing boat, taking pity on us, threw us a line and towed us over the ridge formed by the incoming tide, and away we went out into the channel. Mamma, all atwitter with nerves and anxiety, posted herself on the pier with a bagful of pennies for the telescope, to which she glued her eye, hoping in this way to follow our progress and raise the alarm if anything went wrong.

But we were doing fine, sailing along on the rising tide,

followed by a flock of excited seagulls madly hoping for a quick capsize. John was at the tiller, giving orders in sailing terms which neither Anne nor I understood, so that we kept making stupid mistakes and being sworn at in proper sailor fashion.

After a couple of hours, my mother's pennies having probably run out, she started to make frantic signs for us to return. Obediently, as agreed beforehand, we turned and made for the estuary. But by then the tide was going out, making it impossible for us to get anywhere near the river. Patiently we sailed back and forth, but the enormous rush of outgoing water from the furiously flowing river Arun, combined with the ebbing of the tide, kept us well away, without the slightest chance of getting back before the tide turned again. For several hours we sailed about, each time getting washed far out to sea again. And not until it began to grow dark, and the tide started to rise, were we able to enter the harbour again. That day, we learned a great deal about sailing, but still not quite enough to save us from another idiotic mishap.

Having managed, by a series of flukes and miracles, to miss death by drowning on several occasions, and to survive the entire holidays, John and a couple of his friends decided to sail back to their baronial establishment in Arundel by way of the river. Anne and I wholeheartedly fell in with this scheme and as we formed by then a solid united front on practically every issue, all speaking with one voice, poor Mamma's sensible objections were overruled, and John cajoled Marie into packing his trunk with a minimum of grumbling at the folly of our ways.

Once this was packed and duly bound with several yards of rope, we heaved it on top of a couple of bicycles, and we set off in this fashion, the two friends gripping the handlebars, Anne and I holding the trunk in place and John pushing from behind. We arrived at the harbour without mishap, followed by a group of interested spectators who kindly lent a hand when the time for embarking the cargo came. The loading operations proved more difficult than we expected, as the boat kept springing away like a shying horse, or else leant over sideways, shipping a good deal of water every time we tried to heave the trunk on board.

When this was finally achieved, and all five of us had jumped in and baled out as much water as we could, the tide, now rising fast, tossed the boat up like a nutshell and shot it forward on to a gaily racing wave backed by a brisk offshore breeze. With a flourish, and a great cheering from our friends on the bank, we hurried along up the river towards the bridge, with billowing sails and a great uplift of spirits. Whooping triumphantly and skimming along, we plunged under the bridge, when suddenly there was a fearful jolt and a ghastly crunching sound above, as the boat, bouncing merrily along, suddenly rose on a wave, and the mast, caught between two rafters, speared the bridge from underneath. And there it remained, firmly stuck, while the boat, carried along by the tide, turned slowly sideways, leaning over until it was almost at right angles with the water. Somehow or other we clawed the sails down, fastened the trunk to the centre-board, about the only part of the boat which seemed fairly firm at the time, and frantically baled out while the mast creaked and threatened to snap every second. Our friends on shore jumped into rowing boats to come to our aid, anxious faces hung over the bridge shouting advice, and the bus, stopping overhead, disgorged its passengers to watch the proceedings. But in spite of every effort and all the advice, there we remained, with the mast cleaving to the girders, threatening to splinter as the tide continued to rise, while we, soaked to the skin, continued to bale out until the tide started to turn again. I shall never understand why the mast didn't break, the boat didn't sink, and why we survived death by exhaustion, exposure and pneumonia. But we did.

16

TOWARDS THE END of the summer term, Mamma announced that we would be going to St Georges for the holidays. My father was coming back to Europe to spend a few months with us, and was to meet our train in Marseilles as he had done several years before in the middle of the night. We still looked forward to these train journeys through the night as much as ever, especially with a good thunder-storm crashing all round and forked lightning ripping up the sky from end to end. Continental stations in the days of steam engines had a *je-ne-sais-quoi* which, once experienced, was never forgotten. Clanking into one of these at dead of night with a great rattling of couplings and of brakes and the screech of released steam, Marie would spring to her toes at once, straining out of the window to sniff up the murderous fumes of the great clouds of sulphurous smoke rolling slowly under the roof. She would then whistle up the trolley men, buy ham sandwiches and beer, great slabs of Swiss chocolate and fresh supplies of white pillows, all of which were handed up to her through the open window and chucked into our waiting arms. Dogs whimpered and small children whined as their elders dragged them down the platform, followed by tough little porters belted into their tunics like Russian moujiks.

Having left his ship at Port Said, my father and two of his cronies (it would be going too far to describe them as friends) had sailed round the Greek Islands and crossed the Mediterranean in a small yacht, stopping here and there on the way, and taking three months to do it in.

As our train drew into the station, our excitement grew to fever pitch. We did not really think that such an arrangement would come off, but there, on the platform, to our amazement, stood Papa, aloof, patient and remote as a resigned and elderly camel. Chocolate brown from the tropical sun and his three months' sailing in the Mediterranean, he looked strange, and we were overcome by our customary fit of shyness when seeing him again after several years.

A covey of porters was immediately press-ganged by Marie, who marched off at the head of the column, followed by us, to the appropriate platform, as a train was pulling in to the station. John and I climbed in, expecting the rest of the family to follow, but to our amazement, found ourselves chugging away slowly, leaving them all on the platform, surrounded by the luggage, upon which perched an empty bird-cage, the usual mouse-traps tied together with string, and the two vintage Singer sewing machines. To our surprise, the family watched us go in silence (stunned, I suppose).

And so there we were, just the two of us, without tickets or money, rattling through provincial France at dead of night, having not the slightest idea what to do about it. As far as we knew, the train might be going anywhere, perhaps even over the frontier into Spain, or right across the country into Germany or Austria. After a brief conference, we decided to see how far we could get without being caught and dragged away in chains as stowaways. We thought it safer not to go into a compartment, so we pulled down the *strapontin* seats at one end of the corridor, and dived into the *toilettes* at the first sign of inspector or ticket collector. This worked like a dream—we were still at large at nine o'clock the next morning, when to our amazement we chugged into the little station of Royan. And giddy with lack of sleep and starvation, we were quite convinced it was a mirage, when the identical group we had left behind in Marseilles in the middle of the night was standing before our eyes, beside the pile of luggage, complete down to the last shrimping net. Having caught the next train, they had somehow or other, in a most mysterious fashion, overtaken us during the night, and had already been waiting half an hour for our arrival.

Jacques, who was there to meet us with his father, gave me a bear-hug which squeezed all the air out of my lungs with a loud hiss, and which I bore without protest. I realised how much I had missed him, and it was bliss to be back. They had brought their own cars, and prudently booked several taxis as well, knowing as they did from experience the amount of luggage there would be.

When we reached the Villa Cobalt, which was to be our summer residence, Jacques grabbed me by the hand and pulled me out of the car. We raced down to the beach at breakneck speed, where we flopped down in the dunes under the tamarisk trees. For a while we sat in silence, filled to the brim with utter contentment and peace. I looked around quickly to see if anything had changed, at the little cove where the fishermen let down their nets, at the reef uncovered by the retreating tide, at the *plongeoir* which had so nearly broken my neck, and at the huge sweep of white sand all the way to Suzac. No, nothing had changed. It was all as it had always been.

But it seemed that *I* had changed. 'You look different,' he said, accusingly. 'You've changed.'

'That's all the worry about the exams. Lines and wrinkles,' and I smiled to show that, though wizened, I still *felt* the same.

'I expect you will look better when you are brown,' he said presently.

'That won't take long,' I replied, and we sat in silence, chewing the juicy end of grass stems.

'There is such a lot I want to tell you,' he said after a while.

'Well, there's plenty of time.'

'Yes, there's plenty of time. And now let's go and help Marie with the unpacking. It's not fair to leave it all to her.'

'We' helping Marie meant that he sat on a bed, occasionally shunting an empty trunk out of the way, or heaving a new one forward, into which Marie and I dived, emerging with armfuls of sheets and towels, linen hats, bathing things, first-aid-kit, card games, and all the paraphernalia indispensable to a well-run seaside holiday. Although we did not know it then, this was to be the most wonderful, and the last of all our summers, as the next one was to be swallowed up by the war, which had got going in good earnest by then.

The Villa Cobalt, directly opposite the chalet Gaudin (which was completely engulfed by the tangled vegetation of the garden, and by now very decrepit), was as bare as all the summer villas we had ever occupied, but less smelly, as the 'convenience' had a little hut all to itself in the back yard. The front garden, shaded by mulberry trees, became our studio, where we spent all our time when not on the beach, writing and illustrating our stories. During that summer holiday we discovered Katherine Mansfield's short stories, which Jacques read aloud, and when we had come to the end of her output, somebody produced Rosamund Lehmann's *Dusty Answer*, and we fell under *her* spell for the next few weeks.

To supplement my income of three francs a week, I put a card in the *Bureau de tabac*, to advertise English lessons, and try to catch a few holiday students. This brought me several pupils, and became a modestly lucrative occupation, which swallowed up two hours every morning, and elicited a great deal of grumbling from Jacques, who averred that I was wasting the best time of the day in this useless occupation. We started at eight a.m. as we were all (pupils and teacher alike) keen to get finished as early as possible. One girl who was older than me and knew far more English grammar than I did, had to be kept to conversation only. Her accent was atrocious and always remained so, in spite of our combined struggles. She had no ear at all. One morning, as we sat by an open window toiling with our 'The's' and aitches, a pebble hit me in the small of the back.

Knowing his ways, I guessed that Jacques had arrived, and turning round, saw him standing in the garden, immensely tall and golden brown, square-shouldered and grey-eyed, and quite unconscious of his looks. Suddenly I realised how lucky I was, how much I would miss his solid and reassuring presence, which even made itself felt in his letters, if he were suddenly to disappear. And there and then I made a vow to bear with his moods and his possessiveness, and never to be impatient or uncooperative again. I made a face and said, 'Nearly ready. Won't be long,' and finished the lesson in a new kind of glow. Behind me, I heard him crunching back and forth on the gravel, whistling through his teeth, trying to be patient. When I finally joined him outside, he was in a surprisingly sunny mood. 'You gave me a lovely smile just then,' he said.

'Really?' This *was* unexpected! 'Don't I always smile when I see you?'

'There are smiles and smiles,' he said darkly, and went all gloomy again. I never seemed able to say the right thing. We trudged off to the beach in silence, and it was a relief to find the others already there, giggling over a game of hanging corpse. A great number of small cousins were there too, squabbling and rolling about in the sand. My new-found glow of loving-kindness was already wearing off as I watched Jacques stumping down to the sea to bathe, knowing by the way he walked that he was in a black rage again. Would we never be able to understand each other?

It was not until a long time after, when it was much too late, that I perceived the cause of our malaise. He wanted me to grow up, and enter into an adult relationship with him, a natural wish considering that I was eighteen by then, but immature and backward to an incredible degree, and mulishly clinging to the world of childhood, resisting every attempt to be dragged away from it, the last thing I wanted was to grow up. And so we were hardly ever able to tune in to the same wavelength.

Behind his back, and feeling thoroughly deceitful, I joined in the hanging corpse game without restraint, and was soon rolling about under an avalanche of small cousins, who were determined to tickle me to death.

One fine day towards the end of August, Jacques suddenly decided that we would all go camping. We were delighted with the idea. Mamma's permission was sought, and she readily produced the cash needed to buy tents and equipment. Marie shook her head and darkly prophesied disaster. Such was our excitement that we did not ask her to elucidate, as we usually did, knowing from experience that she was always right, but bustled off instead to buy our gear. So engrossed were we in our intensely exciting lives that we were still completely oblivious of the state of the world, which was hovering on the brink of war. And the grown-ups, in their kindness, did nothing to draw our attention to it, knowing it was going to be *our* war, and realising it would catch up with us soon enough.

The site chosen for our camp was a small, completely deserted sand beach behind the point of Suzac. There, under the overhanging cliff, protected from the West Atlantic winds and facing the rising sun, we pitched our tents. We dug a hole for the fire, and constructed a stone oven above it, and much to our surprise it worked, blazing or smouldering according to our needs. As none of us had ever been scouts or guides, we must have been blessed with beginners' luck.

As the two younger girls, Anne and Ninette, had, much to

their fury, been left behind, Jacques and John occupied one tent, and Nadia and I the other. And around the tents, as protection against unexpected high tides, we erected a wall of dead jellyfish three feet thick. Reinforced with stones and pinned together with sticks, and the whole thickly dusted over with sand, it was a veritable rampart. But in our ignorance, we had reckoned without the stench which would emanate from our defences, so that every morning, retching and choking with nausea, we had to shovel the whole construction away and start again with fresh material—newly stranded jellyfish washed up during the night.

The pine forest came down to the edge of the beach, and provided us with ample supplies of firewood and pine cones. A small stream, trickling down the beach to the sea, heaved and bubbled with elvers, which we scooped up in a strainer and fried in oil like whitebait. The stream also supplied us with fresh water, and the sea was full of shrimps, prawns, crabs, plaice, mullet and sole. And Jacques once wrestled ashore with a baby shark, whose flesh looked and tasted like veal, and was quite delicious. We could have been entirely self-supporting had we not been so greedy and so spoilt. As it was, we craved variety, and good red meat and fresh bread, so that somebody had to trek back to the village two or three times a week to renew our supplies. Normally Jacques and I, renowned as inveterate walkers, were prevailed upon to go. Nadia's ample and voluptuous form was hardly designed for more than undulating between bath and bed, and it was only with the greatest difficulty that we persuaded her to accompany John on one occasion, when Jacques and I longed for a quiet, lazy day on our own, lying in the sun or bathing, as we felt inclined, and with no obligations of any kind. So finally and most reluctantly they set off, John plodding on ahead and Nadia dawdling several yards behind, flip-flopping on the down-trodden heels of her gym shoes.

After they had left, and it seemed unlikely that they would

change their minds and turn back, we decided to get our jobs done early, so that we could relax and enjoy the rest of the day with an easy conscience. We cleaned up the camp and burnt all rubbish on the fire, carted away the dead jellyfish and reeking seaweed, then trailed along the edge of the pine wood, gathering firewood and pine cones, after which we felt we had done our work for the day, and ran into the sea to cool down and wash away the streaming perspiration from our hot faces. The rest of the day was spent as we had planned, lying in the sun between bathes, snoozing and chatting, playing the odd game of hanging corpse (for once he graciously condescended to indulge me in my childish pleasures), and adding a few chapters to the novel of the moment. It was an idyllic day (of which there are only a few in a lifetime) of hot sun, blue skies, warm seas, without a single quarrel or disagreement, and the peacefulness of that little cove was so absolute that its virtue still holds good after all these years, and works its magic again whenever I think of it.

As the sun was setting and John and Nadia had still not returned, we decided to refill our water bottles before dark, and dug them out of the wet sand where they dwelt for coolness. About half a mile away in the heart of the pine wood stood a mysterious monument like the one in Landseer's painting of the Monarch of the Glen, which we had discovered many years before in our early teens, and which we called, heaven knows why, *le tombeau de Napoleon*. This had been built beside our little stream, at a spot where it widened into a shallow pool.

Having sunk our bottles into the water to let them fill themselves, we waded in and sat down in the middle of the pool. If you sat quite still for a few minutes, the floor of the pool would begin to heave and sway, and a multitude of crayfish, after their initial fright at the intrusion, would get up and set off again, resuming their slow and purposeless activities. All you had to do was to pick them up as they waddled past and pop them into the keep-net.

Having secured our supper, and the bottles being filled, we returned to the camp, gathering a few pine cones on the way to revive the fire. By the time we reached the camp, the sun had set over the sea. The plovers and other sea-waders paddled along the edge of the water, shrimping busily, while a cloud of hysterical sea-gulls gigged up and down over a patch of bubbling water, denoting a shoal of sardines. The lime-green sky was dotted with little wodges of apricot clouds, and as a slight breeze coming from the Atlantic had cooled the air sufficiently to make a fire bearable, I scraped away the sand and dropped some cones into the ashes, which I fanned vigorously with the frying pan for a few minutes, until it all crackled into flame. Jacques threw a bundle of twigs into it, and our fire blazed high and comfortingly in the gathering dark.

Then he tripped down to the sea for a quick swim, and returned with a saucepan full of water in which to cook the crayfish. This job I always left to him, as I could *not* bear to watch the poor creatures' slow agony, and although he said that I was *complètement folle*, I always maintained, and still do, that they squeaked and squealed and cried out in the throes of this protracted torture. So I hastily left the scene and dashed down to the sea for a delicious, if cowardly, swim. And only when Jacques called out that supper was ready did I return to the fireside.

Famished as we were, the crayfish tasted very good, and we gobbled the lot, washing them down with great swigs of fresh water from their own stream.

The saucepan being the only item to wash up, I tossed it out of sight behind the woodpile (the 'washing-up' was only done from time to time, when the pan was encrusted with salt inside, and black from wood smoke outside), and we lay down on our bellies by the fire, waiting for John and Nadia to return from the village. We made up a new story to pass the time, each adding a paragraph according to inspiration, for what seemed like hours. And still the other two did not return. Finally, as my eyes would not stay open any longer, I said I was going to bed, and he could wait up for them if he liked. 'Let's go for a last swim,' he said, 'and then we will see. They might come back while we are bathing.'

We slid into the smooth dark water, and swam side by side for a few minutes, but as he was doing his faultless crawl, while I struggled with my own version of the dog paddle (he had long ago given up trying to improve my style), he soon outdistanced me, leaving a trail of phosphorescent froth, in which I was perfectly content to roll and splash about.

Apart from an infinitude of stars which seemed more numerous than usual in the darkness overhead, the air all round was inky black, and the water looked as if it were illuminated from below with green, fluorescent light. After a while Jacques returned and said 'lazybones' as he passed me on his way to the beach. I followed him out. The other two still had not returned, and I said I was going to bed. He kicked sand on to the fire as he rubbed his hair and mopped his face, then we both crawled into our respective tents.

Lying on our air-beds, we chatted for a while through the canvas, but I kept dropping off, my tongue thickened with drowsiness, until he finally said, 'Oh, go to sleep,' and I gratefully did so.

The next morning, I was still asleep when he hauled me out of my tent by the ankles. He had already lit the fire, had a swim and shaved, and netted a saucepan full of shrimps for our breakfast.

Still only half awake, and dazzled by the sun and the glittering sea, I watched him cook the shrimps alive, but had to turn away when they began to jump out of the pan and into the fire.

'I will go and have a quick dip,' I said hastily, to get away from the hideous sight, and diving back into my tent, struggled into my bathing dress, still damp and gritty from the midnight swim.

The tide was rising slowly, and tiny wavelets crept up the smooth damp sand towards the previous day's tideline of shrivelled seaweed and glutinous, disintegrating jellyfish. The water was cool and clear, and a haze promising yet another hot day hovered over the pine trees. I lay on my back, staring up into the sky, rocking slowly on the gentle swell.

'Come on,' yelled Jacques, 'or are you staying out there all day? If you don't hurry I will eat up your breakfast as well as mine.'

This got me out of the water at once, and I galloped up the beach and threw myself on the sand beside him. We picked the shrimps out of the saucepan with our fingers, tossing the heads and shells back into the fire, where they fizzed and sizzled in a most satisfying way. When he had finished he said, 'Try not to sleep on your back tonight.'

'Why ever not? Anyway, how do you know I sleep on my back?' I asked suspiciously. 'Snoring. Hooting like a foghorn, my dear. In fact you woke me up.'

I was furious, and dealt him a savage kick with my toenails.

'Ah, *petite vipère*,' he yelped with pain, and lunging forward, tried to grab me by the ankle, but I slithered out of his grasp and bolted down to the sea.

For the next hour or so, I floated about, watching him moodily going through the 'housework'. This, which we normally did between the four of us, consisted, as usual, in raking the sand around the camp, tidying the woodpile, digging the water bottles out of the sand to check their content, and carting away armfuls of stinking seaweed, jellyfish and any other flotsum deposited by the last tide. Letting him cope on his own, I was determined not to lift a finger to help.

As he was finishing, John and Nadia, bent under rucksacks stuffed with food, appeared round the point, on top of the cliff.

Feeling it was now safe to get out of the water, I skipped back to the camp to welcome them 'home'. Nadia, who had refused to make the return journey on the same day, had insisted on spending the night in St Georges. Her feet, she said, were covered with blisters, and needed attention. Nothing more could be expected of her for the next two days. She ambled down to the edge of the water and stayed there, soaking her feet and staring out over the sea for the rest of the day.

17

SHORTLY AFTER THIS, Mamma and the Darlange parents suddenly appeared one evening out of the pine wood through which they had driven in a station wagon. They looked grim. War had broken out, they said, and we must pack up and return with them at once. '*C'est la guerre.*' It was the first time we heard these words, which were to become an infinitely boring phrase repeated at all times by so many people who seemed to relish them, and of which the English equivalent, no less boring, was 'there's a war on.'

The beginning of the war, I regret to say, made very little impact on us except as far as it affected our own lives. Our interest in it, as far as it went, was entirely selfish. The fact that Poland had been invaded by Hitler's armies confirmed our belief, implanted in our minds by Marie as far back as we could remember, that the Germans were a bad lot, and what more could you expect. It was hard luck on the poor Poles, but how they could be helped by a world war was a profound mystery. It was one of those things you just had to accept, because the grown-ups, who had launched the war, said it was inevitable. And of course they knew what they were doing.

Our own personal fate was greatly improved by it, as my mother, for another unfathomable reason, decided that because of the war, we girls would not go back to school in England, but would remain in St Georges instead. John was sent back to his Baron in Arundel for further cramming, while we were enlisted once more at the Collège de Royan. In spite of the expected bombing raids on Paris, Jacques, whose education was also a serious matter, returned to the capital with his parents, while Nadia and Ninette, to our infinite joy, were left behind with their grandmother and joined us at the college.

Our return to England being cancelled, Mamma nevertheless felt the need for a move of some sort, and we were bundled, along with all our trappings, to the Villa de la Falaise for the winter. This was on top of the cliff, where the fishermen let down their nets at high tide. No flowers grew in front of the house, as the sea, splashing into the garden, killed all growing things before they had a chance. So the real garden was at the back, with borders and flowering trees, and a vegetable plot flourished further down behind a hibiscus hedge.

The summer weather went on and on, and I loved to get up early at the hour when the sun, coming up over Suzac at the far end of the bay, slanted through the morning haze along the whole length of the deserted beach, and the garden was stretching itself awake, shaking off the torpor of the night, with buds opening up and petals unfurling, dew-soaked grasses raising their heads as the heavy drops evaporated, spiders tightened up the slackened threads of their webs, and early birds pounced on the stupid, unwary worms. One morning, as I picked my way around as usual, sniffing the heady scent of damp earth, following snail trails to see where the creatures had come to rest after the night's feed, peering into shrubs to see what was going on, and generally renewing acquaintance with the minute world of the garden, and was walking towards the main gate for my usual prowl along the cliff, I stopped dead in my tracks at the sight ahead of me. There, its paws impaled on the railings, hanging on the gate, was a huge Alsation dog. Shaking all over, I forced myself to approach. It was a beautiful biscuit-coloured beast, its head leaning on one side, with tongue hanging out and eyes rolled up, stone dead. How long had it been there, struggling in agony, before released by death? My insides, unreliable as ever, gave a great heave and I dashed back to the kitchen to collect Marie. *She* would know what to do.

With a set face and spectacles gleaming in the early morning sun, she lifted the dog up while I released his paws from the railings. Together we carried him to the far end of the vegetable garden, where, armed with spades, we dug his grave and laid him to rest. 'Poor beast', Marie said as she grimly shovelled on the last spadeful of earth, 'he must have been chasing a cat and tried to jump over the gate. I *thought* I heard a lot of barking in the night.' '*Mon dieu*!' I gasped, as it suddenly dawned on me, 'I heard it too! But I never thought. . . .' We stared at each other, with a ghastly feeling creeping over us. 'Don't tell a soul,' Marie snapped. 'No use upsetting anybody. He is dead and buried and that is that.' And we returned to the kitchen where she poured a cup of strong black coffee for each of us, to which she added a generous dollop of brandy, the first I had ever tasted. And whenever I drink brandy now it gives me a splitting headache, and the picture of that dog, stiff and impaled on the gate, comes up again.

There was still a whole month to go before Jacques had to return to Paris, as the autumn term of French schools used at that time to start on the first of October. We went for immense walks through the woods, the vineyards, the fields and along the seashore. Those beaches, which stretched for hundreds of miles from the Spanish border almost up to Brittany, increased at an alarming rate every year, as mountains of golden sand, washed up by the Atlantic Ocean, encroached on the plain behind. In order to stop the spread, young pine trees were being planted everywhere along the coast behind the dunes. Sheltered by these growing trees, grazing lands stretched for hundreds of miles all round, which turned into bog in the winter. Here and there a shepherd, cloaked and hooded in a long brown cape, staggering about on his stilts, stalked the land like Frankenstein.

Further inland still, where the old prehistoric forest started, you could walk for miles under the trees without seeing a soul. The great trunks creaked and groaned in the Atlantic winds, and the smell of resin oozing from their bark filled the air, mingled with the smell of mushrooms and damp pine needles.

Sometimes we took sandwiches, and sometimes we stopped at a farm house for bread and cheese and (behind Mamma's back) great jugs of cider, which made my legs wobble. We returned at dusk loaded with mushrooms, wounded birds whose legs or wings had to be set by Marie, blackberries, large seashells, shark's teeth or dog-fish eggs. There were always treasures to be found wherever we went. But I flatly refused to accompany him when he took his gun. This was a completely different type of expedition, when he and his father and uncles left for the marshes before dawn, with all the gun dogs rampaging around.

Towards the end of September, the Equinoctial tides brought torrential rains, as implacable as any monsoon I had ever known. We were confined to the house, which suited me very well, as I was perfectly happy to scribble and paint and pass the time of day playing dotty card games with Nadia and the others. But Jacques, like a caged animal, prowled up and down the drawing-room, growling at the weather, until even Mamma's patience began to wear out and she asked him to sit down and read aloud to us. The book she handed him, *Le Grand Meaulnes*, was a fortunate choice, as it fitted his mood like a glove. We were all mesmerised by the story, and the dreamlike world in which it took place, and the remaining days of our 'last summer' were imbued with the atmosphere of the book to such an extent that whenever I read it again, it feels almost autobiographical. But

Jacques, although temporarily soothed down, began to fret again.

When the deluge eased up a little and settled to a steady downpour, he decided it was time to get out again. As the ground was so 'wet' (running with flood water, actually), we would go on our bicycles. Shrouded in our black *ciré* raincoats and gumboots, we set off one morning into the driving rain with a bundle of sandwiches in our saddlebags. Within a few minutes we were drenched to the skin, the water running down our necks and straight into our boots, which were soon filled to the rim. I pounded on after him, with eyes tightly shut and spirits at a low ebb. I was half thinking of turning back, whatever he might say, when he shouted over his shoulder, 'Come on and don't be so *douillette*. Just imagine you are a fish and you will love it.' Fortunately the wind had dropped and the weather was warm, so I squelched on blindly, longing for it all to be over. The only thing which kept me going was the thought that he, unlikely as it might seem, was probably enjoying it.

After several hours of bumping over ruts and splashing through puddles he called a halt, saying it was time for lunch, and pedalled off the lane along which we were paddling, to a clump of beech trees on the edge of the wood. Hopping off my bicycle, I toiled after him, with water brimming over my wellingtons.

We settled under a dripping tree, sitting back to back in the shallowest puddle we could find. He was as happy as a lark, and disgruntled though I was, I couldn't find the heart to grumble and spoil his pleasure. We unpacked our sandwiches and began to chew the sodden bread in silence.

'You realise,' he said after a while, 'what I ought to do?'

'No, what?' There did not seem much choice at that moment except to endure.

'The proper thing would be for me to kiss you.'

'Good heavens!' I cried in great alarm, 'Surely there's no

need for *that*!'

'No, I don't suppose there is,' he conceded in a reasonable voice, and having finished his own sandwiches he leaned over and scooped up one of mine, which curled over his finger like a wet flannel.

We went on munching in silence for a while, and then he was off again.

'You realise, don't you, that there are only two people in the world who would do anything, absolutely *anything* for you?'

I shifted uncomfortably and asked the question he was expecting.

'Really? No, who do you mean?'

'Me and your mother of course. I sometimes wonder if you appreciate it. You seem to take so much for granted.'

Quite true, I thought, feeling guilty. But I was being offered something for which I was not ready. That much I dimly realised, but could not tell him so.

'Hum,' was all I could find to say. After a while he heaved a great sigh and said, 'Ah well, it will be quite different when we are married. You will see.'

At this point something stirred in the undergrowth.

'Oh, look,' I cried with relief, at the sight of a very wet rat creeping out of a bush and coming towards us. Jacques cheered up at once. 'Poor thing,' he said, 'wet to the skin. Can you give him one of your sandwiches? I'm afraid I've finished mine.'

Mercifully, there was no more of that kind of talk, and soon after, the holidays having come to an end, he returned to Paris, and we resumed our daily bicycle rides to the College.

When winter came at last, it was very cold indeed. Every morning, soon after seven, we set off in the dark, and made our way to Nostram to pick up Nadia and Ninette and a great gaggle of small cousins, eight of whom were now old enough to go to school. The french windows of their dining-room were decorated with a different frost pattern every day. Sometimes it was ferns, and sometimes seaweed, and once it was fireworks. I was never able to discover the cause of this extraordinary variety of design. When I asked, people looked vague, or told me sharply not to be such a bore. And so I still do not know.

The dining-room, steaming hot, smelled of wood smoke and cocoa, and was always in a state of indescribable confusion, with dogs cluttering up the fireplace, coats, scarves and satchels strewn everywhere, and the entire family clustered round the table gobbling up as much breakfast as they could swallow in the short time available. They all talked with their mouths full, frantically learning the verbs or verses which they should have learnt the night before, squabbling and shouting, and trying to get their belongings together. The only two calm faces were those of their grandmother and the Annamese cook, who glided imperturbably around the table with jugs full of cocoa and plates of buttered rolls.

Half past seven was the irrevocable deadline, and we always, somehow or other, managed to set off by then, pedalling furiously down the sea road in the icy wind, our headlights flickering feebly on and off.

Because of the war, and the vast numbers who had stayed behind instead of returning to Paris, school ended blissfully for us at two o'clock, after which the poor *professeurs* had to take on the second batch, who worked from two until eight o'clock at night.

By then I was in the top class, with huge hairy boys of nineteen and twenty in leather jerkins and skin-tight shorts full of intriguing bulges, all immensely polite and urbane, and no more fighting in the school yard. We discussed instead the theories of Kant and Nietsche, and moaned about the intricacies of physics and astronomy. The amount of homework we were given was horrifying, but we soon cut it down when we realised that the teachers never had a chance of marking half of it. So we spent the afternoons sprawling in the drawing-room of the Villa

Falaise, or one of the bedrooms at Nostram, gossiping, giggling or playing idiotic card games which we invented as we went along. Without Jacques to nag and bully us, we were able to be as silly as we liked, and only got down to our homework after tea, with much groaning and grumbling.

And so the days went by most agreeably, and the weather grew colder, and the edge of the sea became encrusted with ice. The war was beginning to make itself felt, and certain things were becoming scarce. Marie had always cut up large lumps of scrubbing soap (*savon de Marseilles*) with a cheese wire, and we were each given a piece of it to wash with. Made for laundry and floorscrubbing, it invariably scorched the top layer of your face off, and roughed up the skin of your hands like a cheese grater. One day, my mother, who had not really looked at any of us for some time, suddenly caught sight of my sore face and said, 'Why is your skin so rough? What have you been putting on it?' She asked suspiciously.

'Just the ordinary soap,' I answered, surprised. 'Why, what's the matter?'

'You look like a crocodile handbag,' she remarked. 'You ought to start using night cream.' Night cream indeed! I was not going to spend any of my precious three francs a week pocket money on such useless, unnecessary stuff. And it was certainly not the sort of thing that Marie was likely to provide. We both conveniently forgot about it, and no more was said. We went on scouring ourselves with *savon de Marseilles*, and it was not until this became one of the commodities in short supply, when soap all but disappeared from the shops, that our complexions lost their crocodile texture and showed remarkable improvement.

Then meat, we were told, was becoming scarce, and the butchers were made to close every other day, with the result that everybody bought twice as much on open days, and the particular minister whose brainwave this had been was foiled on that score.

By Christmas, Marie was drying out used-up tea leaves, to be brewed again a second time. Later, coffee beans were made of roasted acorns, and we gave it up altogether. But on the whole, we cannot be said to have suffered much during that period of the war.

Jacques and his parents arrived on Christmas Eve with some of their cousins who lived in Belgium and had foreseen the coming disasters, in spite of the government's repeated assurances that the Germans would never step over the Maginot Line. The Belgian cousins took over the Chalet Gaudin which, because of its crumbling condition, was the last available house as St Georges was now stuffed to the brim with refugees from the North.

We all gave a hand with the painting and wall-papering, and John did wonders for the woodwork with his hammer and fretsaws, and all the other complicated and nameless tools which by now he used with professional dexterity. And by the end of the Christmas holidays, the Chalet Gaudin was a very desirable residence indeed. It was a strange feeling to be back in our first St Georges villa with all its memories, happy and otherwise (and even worse, when it came to the oysters), and now we had an extra port of call for playing cards, or reading aloud, or painting and writing, or whatever else.

On Christmas Eve Marie bundled us all off to confession. We noticed then, for the first time, that she never went herself, but were far from bold enough to remark on it. So off we went much against our will, and scoffed at by the Darlanges, who were all three confirmed free-thinkers by then.

Inside the box, peering through the confessional gloom to identify his customer, the priest looked at me suspiciously through the little grill, and said severely that he had heard I was engaged. As there seemed nothing wrong in that, I agreed that yes, indeed, in a way I could be said to be engaged. He then asked me quite fiercely, if I was being good. Anybody else of my age would have known what he was driving at, but as I was still churning out the same old sins as ten years before (quarrelled with my sister, told three lies last week instead of the usual one to which I tried to ration myself, gobbled up the last pot of strawberry jam, etc., etc.), he naturally suspected that I was having him on. And of course I was, but not in the way he thought. To keep him happy, I was simply striving to simulate a piety which I did not feel.

When we had all gone to bed, and I was snuggling down under my eiderdown and a pile of coats (the weather was fiercely cold, there was no heating in the room, and anyway I kept my window wide open), a shower of pebbles suddenly rattled on the floor of my bedroom. Then I heard a low whistle, and I knew there was nothing else for it —I had to get out of bed. So out I crept, struggled into one of the coats lying on top of my bed, and padded over to the window. The night was bright as tempered steel, and the moon, like a huge white Camembert cheese pasted onto the Prussian blue of the sky, dispensed an eerie light, so diffused that it cast no shadows. Jacques, who had come for a late-night chat, was standing beneath my window all swaddled up in an enormous muffler. I leant out and said hello, and how nice of him to come, but he mustn't stay as it was so very cold. This alas, did not go down very well, and he went all silent standing there leaning against the wall with an outstretched hand, pawing the ground with one foot. I cursed myself, but could find nothing else to say. It was desperately cold, and I longed for him to go. It would only mean another sore throat, a tight chest, and a week in bed. Oh, why didn't he *go*? A little moan escaped me.

'What did you say?' He looked up sharply.

'Don't they mind what time you come in?' The nearest to a hint that I could make it.

'Oh, no, it's different for boys. They can stay out as long as they like. It's *girls* who have to be in early.' The hell it is, I thought, I might just as well be out good and proper, instead of hanging out of this wretched window. There was another long silence. Suddenly he said, 'You'll be ready at six?'

'Heavens! I will never manage to wake up. It is nearly midnight.'

'Good heavens, so it is. Well, I will come round and throw gravel at your window until you wake up. And please don't be late. I don't want to miss the sunrise!'

'Okay. Goodnight,' I said firmly.

'Goodnight, and you *will* be quick in the morning, won't you?'

It felt as if I had hardly dropped off to sleep when the dreaded shower of pebbles was bouncing on my floor again. At first, as I struggled to consciousness and surfaced from the pile of coats, I thought I was diving through a huge breaker, with the sound of crashing water above me. And then I remembered, scrambled into my clothes and boots, and tried to wash my face, but gave up when I realised that the water was frozen solid in the jug. Rapidly brushing my hair I screwed it into a tight knot which I skewered to my skull with all the pins I could find. As we still had no private mirrors in our rooms, there was no point in even trying to titivate. Creeping through the sleeping house, I grabbed my cloak from the coatstand in the hall and slipped outside, where Jacques was waiting for me.

'You've been ages,' he said. 'We will have to hurry if we want to catch the sun before it comes up. Come on, let's be off,' and grabbing my arm, he dragged me through the gate and out to the cliff path, stalking along with such huge strides that I had to break into a brisk trot to keep up with him.

We covered about five miles at this pace, and by the time we reached the high dune we were making for, I was exhausted, breathless, famished and wondering whether it was really worth all the effort. However, we made it in time, and all was well.

The sandy hill on which we stood was planted with young pines, and the tall grass all round, frozen stiff, stuck out of the ground like knife blades. Standing still and puffing out little plumes of frosted air, we stared expectantly at the orange horizon.

The colour gradually mounted in the sky, picking out little specks of cloud, and spilling out onto the wet sand and mud flats of the bay. The sea was miles out and the tide was still retreating. Flocks of waders picked their way delicately about in the ooze; there were plovers, curlews and avocets, and another kind on high matchstick legs as large as storks which even Jacques could not identify.

The sky changed slowly to geranium red, and then deep ox-blood, and the sun emerged from behind the sea. Jacques heaved a great sigh. It really meant a great deal to him to be present at this daily ascent of the sun, almost as if he did not trust it to do the job properly without his personal supervision.

'Better than any painting in the world, isn't it little one?' I *loathed* being called 'little one', but let it pass.

'Well yes, I suppose so,' I answered, but secretly thought his own confections rather better. He got a greater variety of colour in, and branched out into lovely streaks of lime and primrose which a real sunrise seldom produced. We stood still as the sun slowly climbed out of the sea, and the colour faded in the sky.

'One day we will build a hut here, on this very dune, and we will live like hermits, right away from the world, with nothing but the sun and the sea, and the beach and the sky, and the birds and all the wild things of the woods,' he said.

'Won't it be rather cold, at this time of the year? I mean . . .'

'I will chop down trees (he waved at the saplings around us) and we will have huge log fires. I will fish, and shoot wild duck and rabbits, and you will make clothes for us out of their skins.' *Duck* skin? Unnerved by the cold, a ghastly fit of giggles, as so often happened in church, began to rumble inside me. Mercifully, I managed to keep it down.

[133]

Carried away by his vision, he put his hand on my hair and started to poke about in it. The pins began to rain down past my face. I gritted my teeth, but said nothing. Soon the twist of hair began to slip down the back of my neck, and would be blowing about wildly all the way home. He saw my expression and looked contrite, but it was too late.

'Let's go back before you catch cold,' he said solicitously. 'We will cut across the fields.'

The 'fields', a euphemism for what was normally bogland into which you sank hip-deep, were now frozen stiff into ruts and troughs over which we staggered and stumbled, disturbing volleys of snipe, which I was only able to identify because of their unmistakable zigzagging flight (so I got no marks for that) and hundreds of teal and mallard.

At one point we crossed a frozen pond, and a slow creaking sound, beginning by the sedges, crept all along the edge and a long crack appeared on the ice.

'Run for it,' shouted Jacques, 'Quick, or we'll sink.' We belted across, as the ice slowly began to dip on our side. One enormous leap (M. Coulon's early training came in useful here) and we were on firm, crusty bogland again.

'You realise that if we had gone under we would have drowned, don't you?' he said, as if I were responsible for our near-miss.

We kept going at a good speed, urged on by ravenous hunger now, scuttling across the frozen marshland, scrambling over the dykes, with curlews wheeling above our heads, mewing accusingly. Jacques pointed at something a mile or so up in the air. 'What's that bird up there?' he asked. I looked up, but beyond the curlews, saw nothing in the bland, spotless sky, and made a wild guess, 'A lapwing? a lark?', then seeing the sorrowful look on his face, 'Oh, God, I suppose it's a damn kestrel!' (I really *did* like birds as much as ever, but he sometimes had a knack of putting me against them.)

[134]

'A KITE, not a kestrel! Can't you see the tip of its wings?'

I could not even see the wretched bird, let alone the tip of its wings, and hastily changed the subject.

'Shall we go skating this afternoon?' He brightened up at once.

'Yes, let's do that. Just you and me. We will go to Père Goddard's pond. The ice will be safe there.'

'Good idea. But couldn't the others come too? John and Anne would love it.'

'No. We will slip out while they're having lunch. You know them. The whole afternoon will be gone before they stop eating.'

'They could do without their pudding, just for once. I'm sure they wouldn't mind.'

'Why don't you want us to go together, just the two of us? The holidays will soon be over, and we won't see each other again for another three months.' But 'the others' came after all, and through no plotting on my part. It was Robert, one of the Belgian cousins from the Chalet Gaudin, and the laziest of the entire tribe, who, to our amazement, suggested the expedition. They were all in the drawing-room of the Villa Falaise when Jacques and I returned from our sun-watching expedition, and they were wondering what to do with the afternoon.

'Shall we go to Royan, and have tea at the pâtisserie?' suggested Nadia, with a Gauloise hanging from the corner of her mouth.

'No, it's too expensive. I've no money left this week,' said another. 'Let's go and see Yolande then, she's always good for a slap-up tea.' 'We've seen her three days running. Let's think of something else.' 'Shall we go to the woods and sit in the trees and watch the duck flying in from the sea?'

'And freeze to death! No thank you!'

'Let's go skating then,' drawled Robert in his lazy voice. He was lying on his back in an armchair with his feet stuck up on the chimney piece. We all stared at him unbelievingly, and he was already regretting his suggestion.

'Yes,' shouted everybody. 'We'll go to old Goddard's pond. The ice is very thick there.'

Jacques banged a book on the table and stamped out of the drawing-room.

After lunch, John, Anne and I (we had all given pudding a miss) trooped over to Nostram and tapped on the french windows of the dining-room. As Jacques had predicted, the entire tribe were still at table, eating and talking at the same time. We sat by the fire with the dogs, and waited for them to finish. Jacques, appearing with his skates over his shoulder, grabbed me by the arm. 'Come on,' he hissed. 'It will be ages before they finish. Let's get away.'

We plodded off in the direction of Père Goddard's land. It was bitingly cold, but a thin sun managed to light up the sky a little, and made the icicles glitter on the blackberry bushes.

Reaching the pond, we sat in the snow and changed into our skating boots. A few distracted coots scuttled crazily among the bulrushes looking for a hole in the ice, and at the far end a group of mallard stood perched on one foot, brooding and patiently waiting for the thaw. Flights of wild geese were wheeling inland from the mud flats where they had been feeding all day. Jacques eyed them as they landed, and muttered something about his gun. But thank goodness he had left it behind. I could not *bear* to have to retrieve the bleeding, twitching corpses.

Holding hands, we staggered onto the pond and skated along, in and out of the bulrushes, disturbing the birds and testing the ice. As it was quite firm, we set off towards the middle, Jacques going like a maniac and dragging me after him. I cried for mercy and told him to let go of my hand. He turned round and said, 'Am I going too fast? I always forget about your short legs,' and slowed down for a minute, but would not let me go. He soon speeded up again, so that I, unable to keep up, fell flat on my face. Stopping in his tracks, he knelt down and whipped the scarf off my head: 'You will have to sacrifice that,' he said, mopping up the blood which was trickling down my chin.

At that moment the voices of the others could be heard coming through the woods. They had collected quite a few extras on the way, and it was a cheerful, noisy crowd which joined us on the ice.

Scrambling to my feet and leaving Jacques on his knees holding the blood-stained scarf, I flew into the midst of the laughing, shouting throng. We chased each other with shrieks and squeals, and altogether made such a din that Père Goddard, attracted by the noise, suddenly appeared among the bulrushes, his beard bristling with fury.

'Get off my pond at once. Away with you. I gave permission for two or three of you to skate here, but I didn't say the whole village could turn up and trample my crops.'

'What crops, in the middle of the pond, you old nitwit?' sniggered one of the young bloods.

'I'll give you what crops! You just wait,' roared old Goddard, picking up a stick and stalking onto the ice. We scrambled to the other side, where the mallard flew up in alarm.

'If I see you here again, I'll beat you to a pulp, every one of you. Pick up your junk and get off my land.'

He really was in a rage, the silly old fool. There was nothing for it, and we had to leave. I kept well away from Jacques, whose face looked like thunder all the way home. When we reached Nostram, he thawed a little and said, 'Come in and have tea. You needn't go home yet,' and he generously included John and Anne in the invitation.

Nine small faces were munching in silence around the vast dining-room table. This silence, so unexpected from the usually tumultuous small fry, surprised us considerably. It turned out that they were all sickening for measles, and the poor things spent the rest of their holidays in bed, in the dark, in case of blindness.

We went to the sideboard and helped ourselves to cocoa and cake, and large slices of rye bread and butter. Pots of honey and blackberry jelly were dotted about the table. A dozen or so gun-dogs lay in front of the fireplace, with their noses poked right into the ashes. From time to time fleas hopped from one dog to another like circus riders changing horses.

We squeezed in among the ailing ones, and Nadia related our adventures of the afternoon. Her grandmother, serene and com-posed, sat at one end of the table, while facing her was the other old lady of the house, who had been somebody's godmother in the distant past. Fluttering and dainty and full of little exclama-tions, she had lived with the family as far back as anyone could remember. With only two living-in domestics, these two ladies between them ran the house, which sometimes sheltered up to thirty beating hearts, not counting the dogs.

With markedly less enthusiasm than usual, the young cousins nibbled their slices of bread and honey, and sitting beside Jacques, watching them, I loved them all so much, every one of them, down to the minutest midget, the infamous two-year old Antoine (who, when annoyed with someone, lurked around until they had gone for a swim, then peed in their shoes), that my chest positively ached. Quite overpowered by the feeling, I put my hand on Jacques' knee. Unused to such demonstrations of affection he turned round in surprise. 'Are you all right?' he asked anxiously.

'Yes, quite all right, but I think we ought to go.'

He walked back with us, and we sang *Malbrouk s'en va-t-en guerre* all the way home, as we crunched along the frozen beach under the white moonlit sky.

The next two days brought a change in the weather, as a mild West wind blowing in from the far reaches of the Atlantic sprinkled a fine drizzle over the frozen land, thawing the ice in the marshes and enabling the wild duck to get at their water again.

It also made it much easier to get up at dawn when the pebbles came flying in through my window. On the third day the wind had changed to gale force, but the sunrise expeditions were not abandoned for so little.

When we reached our sand dune, with the wind lashing around us like a whip and the sun had duly risen, Jacques said: 'Let's get into that hollow. It should be more sheltered there.'

We jumped into a kind of sandy bunker at the foot of a great pine tree whose branches bounced about like a captive balloon straining on its leash, while it creaked and groaned all the way down its trunk like the mast of a ship.

Out of the wind, it was really quite warm, a real little sun-trap and as cosy as could be. Wood-pigeons, annoyed at being blown out of their trees, complained persistently, while lap-wings and plovers pecked around us like domestic fowl.

'Why don't you lie down?' Jacques said. 'We can do a bit of sunbathing,' and we stretched out side by side. It was delicious. I closed my eyes and basked luxuriously.

Suddenly and without warning, he bent over and kissed me. I sat up with a jolt, and our foreheads clashed together like fighting stags. Taken by surprise, I leapt away in fury. 'How dare you trick me like that!' I yelled, with tears of rage shooting out of my eyes. 'Now you've spoilt everything!' And I stumbled away, making for home as fast as I could in that confounded wind, scattering the birds as I went. It was a very sullen walk home. And I would not speak to him for the rest of the day. He had indeed spoilt everything. After that I was much more wary, and would not go on walks with him any more. Poor John, whom he bored to death with his grievance, finally came to me and said, 'For God's sake, can't you be decent to him again? Aren't you making a lot of fuss about nothing? What's wrong with a kiss anyway?'

'It's not the kissing so much as the way he did it. He tricked me. It was a mean thing to do,' I said, still feeling sore.

'Well forget about it, do, and make friends again.'

'All right, I will. But you can tell him that I am not going to put up with any of that soppy stuff again. And that is *that*!' So the old relationship was resumed (or almost, I still could not bring myself to trust him entirely) and the walks along the sea-shore collecting shells, spotting birds, and even fishing, were resumed.

After John had gone back to England and Jacques to Paris with his parents, my conscience began to nag me about the war, as we had not given a thought to the poor men who had spent Christmas burrowing underground in the Maginot Line. So I went to visit the Knitting Ladies Committee to offer my services. Mamma's contribution to the First World War had been shred-ding linen to be used as lint by the field hospitals ('charpie', as it was called), and I hopefully asked if I might do the same, but was told with much scorn that such primitive and unhygienic methods had long ago been abandoned, and if I wanted to help, I must go and knit; which I did. In the fullness of time, I handed in the fruits of my labour, in the shape of two khaki socks of unmatching size and with lumpy heels, and was advised from then on to stick to mufflers. And so I applied myself to this, producing long, narrow string-like scarves which could not possibly have kept any neck warm.

18

WITH THE SPRING came, suddenly and without warning, the beginning of the end. The first blow leading up to the complete annihilation of France was struck on May tenth with the invasion of Belgium. This trap, craftily devised by the Germans, worked according to plan. The B.E.F., backed by the first and seventh armies, swept forward to the defence of Belgium, thus making it possible for the Panzer divisions, breaking through on the River Meuse where least expected, to rush up behind the Allied Forces, surrounding them and cutting the French army in two.

I am convinced that the reason why France lost the war of 1940 was due to the same causes which brought about her defeat at the Battle of Agincourt. The knights of old who, once immured in their ponderous armour, thought themselves invincible, did not realise, any more than did the French army in 1940 with their heavy, slow-moving tanks, that their equipment was obsolete and quite useless in the face of the fast-moving, up-to-date methods of the enemy.

Relying on the so-called impregnability of the Maginot Line, and still thinking back to trench warfare, the French High

Command were completely taken by surprise by the lightning attack of the Panzer divisions which, once having got through the defences, thundered along to the sea, mowing down any opposition in their path.

Too late, the Allied Forces in Belgium realised what had happened, and Hitler announced with insane glee that he had fooled the West.

Calais fell on May twenty-sixth, and the next day Churchill ordered the evacuation of the B.E.F. The world held its breath during the next nine days, while under fierce bombing from the Luftwaffe, 338,000 men were embarked in every possible kind of craft which came floating over from England, and the miracle of Dunkirk was accomplished. At the time we did not believe a word of all this, thinking that it was only one more story put out by the Government to boost the morale of the country, until we heard Churchill praising the help provided by the R.A.F. saying, among other things, that 'twelve aeroplanes have been hunted by two, one aeroplane was driven into the water and cast away by the mere charge of a British aeroplane which had no more ammunition.'

On June tenth came the 'stab in the back', when Mussolini declared war on France and we were told that there would be 'fighting to the last' at the Somme and Aisne rivers, and when these battles were lost, organised resistance was over, and Paris was declared an open city. After this the Germans spread like wildfire towards the Channel and the Atlantic coast, and on June thirteenth, when Churchill made a surprise visit, the French Prime Minister asked to be let off his undertaking not to make a separate peace with Germany.

Thousands of refugees were flooding through St Georges all day and all night, each one bringing fresh rumours, so-called news of the latest captured town, stories of dive-bombings and shooting-up of the long columns of civilians trudging south along the roads, and the 'fifth columnists', French traitors supposedly in the pay of the enemy, were spreading panic everywhere.

We offered to help, and soon found ourselves in charge of the Citizens' Advice Bureau, handing out blankets, cups of acorn coffee, and trying to find sleeping accommodation for the homeless rabble. People, having walked hundreds of miles, arrived pushing prams stuffed with saucepans and suitcases and exhausted scruffy babies. Lines of cars and horse-drawn carts, loaded with wardrobes, armchairs and potted plants (it was extraordinary what people in the panic of the moment regarded as their most treasured possessions, on no account to be left behind!) crawled through the streets, and nowhere were food or petrol to be found. Wounded soldiers, done up in dirty, blood-stained rags (far less hygienic than my despised 'charpie'!) hobbled in, begging for aspirin and *un petit cognac*, having long ago lost their regiment, saying that the enemy were fifty, thirty, twenty kilometres away. And nobody had any idea what was happening, or where they were going.

Marie, who 'knew' the Germans, said they would rape the girls at once, and we must all be put into glasses and scrape our hair back in rubber bands, then bestowed into the attic for extra safety. Nadia and Ninette, with their smooth brown faces and flirting eyes, were considered to be in greatest danger, although even Anne and I, straight-haired and scrawny though we were, need not think ourselves safe either. As my sole acquaintance with this fate was the Rape of the Sabines, the whole topic seemed lunatic and unreal.

As it turned out, the Germans' moral behaviour when they arrived was impeccable, but later they shot one of the young cousins, aged fourteen, on the suspicion of his having dabbled in the Maquis.

When the loud-speaker on the Place du Marché officially announced that the German tanks were at La Rochelle, poor Mamma, who was quite distracted, went to see the mayor for advice.

[143]

'Get out,' he shouted at her. 'Get out immediately. I will give you all the petrol you want so long as you go. I don't want any British here when the Germans arrive. I don't want any trouble.'

And so Jacques' father, collecting our petrol ration from the Town Hall, said he would drive us to Le Verdon, on the opposite side of the estuary, where American troops had landed during the First World War, and where a British destroyer now lay at anchor, to gather up any stray Britons still left behind on French soil. At eleven o'clock, just before we were to set off, the destroyer was struck by a torpedo, and disappeared from view within half an hour. There was no point in going to Le Verdon now. The only thing to do was to drive to Bordeaux, where the British Consul would take us under his wing. Jacques was to come with us to London, where he would join the Free French Forces of Colonel de Gaulle.

And now comes the most painful episode that I have had to write so far: Mamma announced that only British subjects, holding United Kingdom passports, would be repatriated to England. How she knew this I have no idea—but as it turned out she was right as far as civilians were concerned. And so Marie, with her Swiss passport, *would have to be left behind*! We were thunderstruck. In a passion of rage and grief we turned on my mother, and said many terrible things which I, for my part, much regretted later. We were no better, I told her bitterly, than a bunch of rats leaving a sinking ship; that our duty was to stay on and carry out as much sabotage as we could until the Germans were finally defeated, and that leaving Marie behind was the basest deed ever perpetrated by any human being. And many other things as well, dreadful, shameful things which only an adolescent suddenly plunged for the first time into the hell-hole of utter desolation and despair is capable of saying.

All the afternoon we inched along the road to Bordeaux in bottom gear, hemmed in on all sides by thousands of refugees, fleeing they knew not where. The June sun blazed down on the crawling mob and the noise and the heat were unbearable. Mamma had insisted, as we could take no luggage, that we should each wear two skirts and jumpers, and we sweltered painfully, while Christine, who was not quite eight, cried all the way monotonously calling for Marie. It seemed as near a nightmare as real life could ever be. Dusk fell without the suspicion of a breeze, as the heatwave stretched into the night. On the edge of a small village, whose name I shall never forget, St Jean de-Cubezac, overcome by the heat and the general horror of the situation, the car broke down completely and refused to go further. Leaving it by the roadside, we walked to the *auberge* at the entrance of the village, and there met with luck for the first time that day. The *patronne*, who was astonishingly affable, said yes, we could all spend the night in her attic if we didn't mind sleeping on the floor, or object to mice and prowling owls who swooped in at night to hunt the mice. This sounded to us like a corner of paradise, and we gratefully accepted her hospitality. It was after midnight when Jacques, Christine and I toiled up the attic stairs, while my mother was trying to wheedle a loaf of bread out of the management. But there was no food about, not even at black market prices any more, and apart from a few plums which we managed to buy in the morning, we had to go hungry for the next three days.

The attic window, wide open as it was, formed a perfect frame for the spectacle of a burning town in the distance: Bordeaux was on fire. We rushed to the window. Christine, who was so tired that she had only just managed to make the stairs, gripped the window sill and jumped up and down with excitement.

'Look,' she yelled, 'look, fireworks! Lovely fireworks!' and she leant far out, balancing on her stomach to get a better view. Clutching her by the waist, I dragged her back. From where we stood, we had a sharp, clear view of the bombardment. Zooming and sweeping in circles, the German bombers, lit up from below by the glow of the burning town, looked like gigantic fireflies. 'Oh, dear God!' Jacques groaned. 'What are we going to do? Whatever is going to become of us?'

I looked at his perplexed, uncomprehending face, at Christine struggling in my grasp, and thought of my great grandfathers who had so confidently set out over a hundred years ago from the town which was now smouldering like a jungle fire under the sticks of bombs falling out of the sky, and of Marie whom we had abandoned to her most hated enemy in her old age, and of the thousands of homeless people all over the country frantically fleeing from the invading armies, and I knew that whatever *was* to become of us, the time had come, irrevocably, for us to grow up, and that our childhood was now over forever.